ETERNAL JOURNEY

———◆———

A Parable of Love, Loss, & Renewal

*Carol, Hutton
APHS, Class of '66*

CAROL HUTTON, ED. D.

———◆———

Beach Publications

ISBN: 0-9662-088-0-3
Library of Congress Catalog Card Number 97-94990
Book Design: InterMedia
Published by: Beach Publications
Printed in the United States of America

For mail orders, contact:
        Beach Publications
        P.O. Box 812228
        Boca Raton, Florida 33481

        561-483-2817
        beachpub@juno.com

For courageous souls everywhere
who are searching for meaning in loss
and for those who help them

In loving memory of my mother, Charlotte, the true storyteller
in our family. It was my mother who first read to me;
it was my mother who told me my first story. My mother,
through her stories - fact, fiction, and folklore - taught me about
life and loss with the insight of a psychologist, the guidance of
a teacher, and the wisdom of a mystic. Her gift for finding
meaning in seemingly meaningless pain and suffering
continues to inspire and humble me.

Acknowledgments

No project results from one person's effort, and *Eternal Journey* is no exception. I could not have seen this endeavor through without the energy and support of many, many people. There are a few individuals who made unique contributions to the work.

Thank you to Patti Cleary, the editor who connected with me through my professional network. Patti read one of the first drafts of the manuscript while on her vacation, and gave freely of her time in the early part of my journey. Her honest, yet supportive feedback gave me confidence to go the distance. Patti re-connected with me and *Eternal Journey* and served as the final editorial consultant on the project. She brought insight, enthusiasm, and patience at a time when I was short on all three. She coached, mentored, cajoled, and challenged me to better performance. Through her example, I came to a new respect for the craft of both writing and editing.

There were a number of other experienced writers and editors who read drafts of the manuscript at varying stages of its development. Thank you to Susanna Barciella and Harriet Forman, both talented editorial writers who also critiqued early drafts of the manuscript, and to Sharon Geltner Schwartz, the editor who worked with me midway through the project. Sincere thanks to Vanessa Reynolds, Mary Lynn Swartz and Dorothy Powell for patiently proofreading the finished manuscript.

I wish also to acknowledge the design consultants at InterMedia, Elyse Murphy and Catherine Cady, whose enthusiasm and talent created the graphics that add beauty and meaning to Anna's story. A heartfelt thank you to my friend, Bonnie Eyler, whose photograph of Gay Head serves as the cover for the book, and to my friend, Patricia King, whose sketch of the Edgartown Lighthouse graces the background of the *Reflections*.

Finally, thank you to the more than one hundred friends and colleagues who read and loved *Eternal Journey*, encouraging me to get it into print. You know who you are. It was your energy that sustained and renewed mine through a project that seemed eternal at many junctures!

Contents

Introduction

There is no coming to consciousness without pain.
C. G. Jung

Stories are the threads that weave and mesh the fabric of our lives. We have been learning from stories for centuries. Mothers and fathers tell them to children, teachers to students, politicians to constituents, leaders to followers, clergy to congregants, and enlightened masters to those who will listen. Stories are the heart and soul, the oral history and legend of families and communities, cultures and nations. It is through our stories that we record, sustain and disseminate our beliefs and values, our pain and our joy. Stories teach and nourish us. They evoke images and feelings that help us learn. Some stories help us heal.

In my work I listen to a lot of stories. For over 25 years, my career has been to help people, first as a nurse, now as an organizational consultant. As a nurse, I assisted patients as they battled physical and emotional changes, struggling with pain and loss. In my years as a consultant, I have traveled both the country and the globe, working with people as they encounter changes in responsibility and function.

My work also offers me opportunities to tell stories, usually to illustrate a point, clarify an issue, or provoke a thought or feeling about the subject at hand. But it is the listening that has often saddened me, angered me, and yet at times, lightened my heart and lifted my soul. Some of the stories have brought tears to my eyes and pained me. Others have made me smile. Each story brings me closer to understanding our human and individual nature, yet leaves me with questions I continue to ponder.

During a break in my consulting practice, I contemplated all the stories I have listened to, remembering clients and patients whose lives have intersected with mine. As all the stories I have heard over these years merged with my own, I realized how universal our experiences on this earth are. Contemplation led to reflection, and *Eternal Journey* came to life.

Early in 1996, I rather impulsively bought a property on Martha's Vineyard Island. Soon after, my sister joined me for a few days to help prepare the house for the season. One gorgeous, crisp, and sunny afternoon, we took a ride out to Chappaquiddick. As we, were driving down the dunes, my sister asked the unexpected. What would I do once I retired? From out of nowhere, I heard myself respond that I wanted to write. As I was reeling from my own words, my sister asked if I would write business or health care books.

"Oh no," I said, "I'd write about relationships."

Five weeks later I was on my way to the island again. On the flight, I sat next to a very pleasant older woman, who initiated a conversation with me. It turned out she was a nurse as well. We swapped stories and experiences, filling in the minutes of the flight. Just before we landed, she told me she was staying at her daughter's home. Her daughter had just written a murder mystery set on the island. Again, out of the blue, I found myself saying, "I'd like to write a book too, but I would never be able to write a mystery. I'd write about relationships."

My lovely companion in the skies said, "I'd read a book like that. You should write it."

So, I suppose you could say *Eternal Journey* began on Martha's Vineyard.

We all know that loss and pain are inevitable in life. Many of us accept that both are integral to our development as human beings. After all these years of listening to stories, I know that each of us has at least one experience that has wounded our heart or soul. The searing pain of loss either burns a hole that can fester in our psyche or illuminates a pathway to our soul. That is just the way we are made.

However you came to read *Eternal Journey*, please know you've been drawn to this story for a purpose. It is not a story for just anyone. It is a parable for those who seek some understanding in their lives, a special story for those who are willing to explore the pain of loss in the belief that only by embracing pain is it released. *Eternal Journey* bridges the physical and metaphysical, the psychological and the spiritual, the rational and the mystical. It is a crossover from pain to joy, loss to hope, fear to understanding, and logic to faith.

Eternal Journey will speak to you in a very special way if you will give yourself the gift of silencing your mind so you can hear your soul. It is a story filled with messages for you and your life. It will leave you with thoughts and feelings that will open your mind and heart so you can begin to contemplate the meaning of loss and pain in your life. And if you are willing to reach both into and beyond what you think and feel, you will gain an understanding from within and beyond, that will guide and comfort you as you continue on your journey through this life.

When reading *Eternal Journey*, listen for the soft whispers of your soul. You may find some answers as you search for meaning in your life.

I hope my story helps you heal.

Carol Hutton
Boca Raton, Florida

The Abyss of Loss

he wind stung Anna's tear-stained face and mouth, causing her lips to crack. She could taste blood as she bit down hard to ward off tears as she placed the single peach rose on the coffin. Her breath was coming in small, painful gasps now, and panic began to set in. She forced herself to watch as Beth was lowered into the cold, hard ground. Chest constricted, hoping to find something or someone else to focus on, her eyes rested on Tom. He looked so old, and so tired. For a brief moment she thought she might be okay. As she turned toward the car, the sobbing began - those awful, audible, embarrassing sobs where your nose drips, you moan and almost vomit.

"Beth, Beth," she repeated to herself. "This isn't happening." As if grief were choking her heart, her chest so tight she could hardly breathe, she put her face in her hands and wept uncontrollably. A disembodied hand took hers, guiding her to the back seat of the limousine. This was all she would remember from the funeral. Despite the many times Anna went over it in her head in the weeks following, she could not remember anything else from that day.

And so her best friend, Beth, was laid to rest. Funny, smart, loyal, pretty, kind and unassuming Beth. Two years earlier, she had called Anna on a Sunday morning to find out about alternative treatments for advanced breast cancer. For Anna, that was the beginning. The beginning of this unrelenting pain and anguish, the beginning of what felt like the end.

Beth O'Neill, Anna thought, was the better half of the duo who had suffered through twelve years of nuns and catechism, rosaries and incense. They had shared a childhood, survived adolescence, and sailed through college and graduate school together. Beth had been her playmate turned soulmate since grade school. Beth and Anna grew even closer through their adult years, despite shifting priorities of husband and children, careers and success. They'd joke about how they would be reunited in old age, rocking on the porch of the retirement home, boring the young attendants with stories of their youth.

Cancer had changed everything once again.

Unbelievably, Beth was the third of Anna's friends to die. Anna had become obsessed over cure rates and cancer statistics. Three friends in as many years, all gone. But numbers and life expectancy statistics meant nothing anymore. Cruel chance did. The scientific, analytical side of Anna, which served her so well as a psychologist, insisted that all three friends should have lived. They should have been among the 90 to 95% in the "cure" category. But they weren't.

Another side of Anna, the deeper, more private aspect of her character, could not, could never get over the multiple tragedy of lives cut short. She berated their fates. Her friends should have been among the survivors, enjoying many more years of life, according to the "experts." Instead, they were sent to early graves. Anna could not reconcile what logically should have happened with the actual, horrible reality. Juxtaposing the two in her mind was simply too much to bear.

The first loss of a friend was hard, the second even more so, but it was Beth's death that shook Anna to her core. Beth had been very special. She and Anna had a connection that defied explanation. It just wasn't fair that she had to die. Why should Beth be the one to suffer and leave this world?

At first Anna was too tired to be in touch with her feelings, but soon she became angry. Her heart ached for her friend, Tom, Beth's husband of twenty years. It didn't seem possible that he was now alone. Anna kept picturing his lost and tired eyes staring at her as the coffin drifted into the earth. She worried how Beth's daughters would cope. Anna felt inadequate and weak as she reached out to them. Once alone, however, Anna began to feel the depth of her own loss. Her heart was heavy with sadness that struck like a clap of thunder and remained like a cloud blocking the light of day. Her best friend's death created a cavern of emptiness in her soul. This black hole of loss and grief frightened her. She felt lost and unfocused, no longer whole. Anna was adrift in a tumultuous sea of pain.

Anna's mother used to say that bad things always happened in threes. Somehow knowing that this trilogy of pain, these three deaths were over now did not make Anna feel any better. In fact, she felt worse. Much worse.

2

The Journey Begins

hree weeks later, the small plane lifted off the tarmac in LaGuardia like a kite caught in a powerful gust of wind. Anna hated these short commuter flights, but this time she hadn't even given it a thought. As the plane began its ascent, Anna became hypnotized by the sight of her own reflection in the window. She watched as the features of her face gradually blended into the white backdrop of floating clouds.

Mesmerized by the stark emptiness of the cloud screen that formed before her, Anna's eyes locked like a laser on the vision that appeared. She sat transfixed as a replay of Beth's funeral appeared in the skies. Anna recalled how Beth had agonized to accept her losses, how she had struggled to embrace her fate. Somehow from the depths of her own solitude and pain, Beth managed to give strength and energy to all around her. As Anna sat gazing into the heavens remembering her friend, she wondered why she had been spared, why she was the one left.

Why?

Abruptly, the little plane sputtered, then jolted as the engine thrust in its effort to reach cruising altitude. Despite the turbulence, noise, and violent vibrations, Anna was mindful only of her loss and its injustice. As the small plane climbed higher and found smoother air, the vision before her eyes melted into a vast emptiness, causing her very being to relax. Anna's mind first drifted, then flowed. She felt transported in time and space.

At first Anna thought it was the pilot trying to make himself heard over the whine of the propellers. But like clouds that pull apart in the sky, the sounds became clearer and very distinct. Anna heard a calm and gentle voice at the funeral, softly reading the words Beth had written in her final days:

"Thank you, my loving husband, my beautiful daughters, my devoted friends, for giving me such a blessed life. I have tried to leave some part of me for each and all of you. As I reflect on my life, I realize that if I had gone back in time, perhaps I could have altered the course of my existence. But I know now I wouldn't have changed anything about my life. The cancer brought me to an awareness that perhaps I would not have acquired without it. My legacy for each of you is to remember to live in the moment..."

As Beth's words faded from her consciousness, Anna realized she was looking down through tears on the island's distinguishing aerial landmark, Oyster Pond. Soon Anna, like the small plane, once again touched the ground. As they rolled down the runway, Anna stared at the rickety, weather-beaten terminal, her mind numb. She would have sat there all afternoon, transfixed upon the small, faded wooden building, if not for the gentle tap on her shoulder. "It's time to go," she heard over her shoulder. With a slight shudder, she came out of her reverie, made a feeble attempt to smile at the man, and gathered her things.

Some find the antiquated building which serves as the terminal for the Vineyard Airport charming. The building was so ramshackle, the baggage "system" so simple, Anna usually found herself chuckling as she collected her bags. No laughter today, however. Anna scanned the parking lot filled with vans and jeeps, anxiously looking for a familiar face. She felt another tap on her shoulder, and turned as the man from the plane asked her if she needed help with her bag. Just as she was about to answer, Anna spotted the metallic silver-blue, four wheel drive with Patrick's friendly face grinning out at her. She managed a weak smile for the stranger, shook her head, and slowly walked towards the Explorer. Patrick, the caretaker for the house where she'd be staying, helped her stow her bags. Few words beyond the perfunctory greeting were exchanged between them as they headed west for the short drive to Tisbury.

3

As If She Had Never Left

artha's Vineyard Island is the larger and more accessible of two sister islands off the Massachusetts coast. Popular as both a retreat and playground, the island bustles each summer with celebrities and families alike. Anna couldn't think of a better place to be at this moment in her life. She had fallen in love with the island the first time the ferry had dropped Beth and her in the little town of Vineyard Haven the June after they had graduated from college.

That was the first time this duo from the tidewaters of Maryland's Chesapeake Bay had visited the rocky shores of Cape Cod. The idea had been proposed by Rebecca, or Becky as nearly everyone called her, a long-term friend from college. She had met them at the bottom of Water Street with Michael, her boyfriend turned fiancé, by her side. They had a great time, that week back in 1970. Somehow, during those seven days, they remembered only the good things that happened during their four turbulent years at the University of Maryland. For that one week, no one talked about the war in Vietnam, its stupidity or tragedy. No one brought up the recent political skirmish, turned tragedy, at Kent

State, which had cast a pall over the already shaky graduation ceremony at their school and across the nation.

They had stayed in a rooming house, later to become a bed and breakfast, sharing a bathroom and shower down a long and crooked hall. They bicycled all over the island, discovering its nooks and hideaways, delighting in its natural charm. Anna, in particular, couldn't get over how it was possible to breakfast in a 17th century whaling village, spend all morning on the beach, then cycle along remote country roads in the afternoon. Years later, after all in the college crowd had established good careers, they could afford annual reunions on the island each June. Becky and Michael had built a summer home in Tisbury, near Lake Tashmoo, in 1991. The get-togethers lasted only three summers, however, permanently interrupted by the cancers that began to take friends one by one.

As she sat quietly in the Explorer, Anna stared at the starkness of the terrain. She remembered that wonderful week from so long ago, a week that marked a major transition in all of their lives. Anna fidgeted with her gloves as her mind tried desperately to grasp all that had changed since then. The war and Kent State were now history. Cancer, not guns, was now slaying her generation.

Anna hadn't been to the island since she and Beth impulsively hopped the ferry one October morning a year ago, and ended up staying a week. Beth had just completed her third and final round of chemo. The cancer had returned earlier that fall, and Beth had reluctantly agreed to put herself through another six weeks of treatment. They stayed at Becky's house that time, too.

Lost in thought, she was oblivious to the barren late autumn landscape as Patrick navigated west on the road to Tisbury. Before she knew it, they were turning onto Lambert's Cove Road, and it seemed as if the tall trees were closing in on her. It was mid-afternoon, with just a hint of sunlight left, and the woods were eerily quiet. The tires crunched somewhat forebodingly on the hardened dirt road, alerting Anna that they had reached the house. Patrick opened the kitchen door, politely asked her if she needed anything, and quietly departed.

The house looked and smelled as it did a year ago. It was as if she had never left. Anna almost expected Beth to come bounding through the kitchen to greet her, but there was only silence and empty rooms. Anna sighed deeply, ambling over to the counter to smell the flowers and read the accompanying note from Becky.

"Hope the weekend alone is really what you need. Patrick has taken care of everything, including stocking the fridge. We're only a phone call away. We love you! Becky & Michael."

"God, I hate that 'we' stuff," Anna mumbled aloud. "Michael can barely stand to be in the same room with me, let alone love me."

Becky and Michael had been part of the crowd forever. A couple since their early college years, they had married the September after graduation. Both of them were equally superficial and pretentious. Yet their boring consistency and their cluelessness about anything real kept Anna intrigued. Each of them was as bland as Anna was intense, as proper as Anna was irreverent, and as predictable as Anna was spontaneous. They were the type of people that, if Anna met them today, she would find absolutely revolting, and vice-versa. Michael had established a very successful practice as a cardio-thoracic surgeon in Fairfield County, Connecticut. The practice, like its location, was among the most affluent in the nation. He never let an opportunity go by without making some deprecating comment about psychologists. Little did he know that his arrogance and insecurity were the catalyst for Anna's first book. Like her husband, Becky was very bright and quite business-savvy. Anna was continually amazed at how much Becky managed to juggle. Between handling a man as high-maintenance as Michael as well as the social demands placed upon her, she had developed a very successful interior design company in the twenty years since graduate school. Becky, ever-pleasant and overly accommodating, would try to take care of Anna too.

It made no sense really, but Anna and Becky had remained friends. It was so illogical that Anna had long ago given up trying to understand the relationship. While she found Michael almost amusingly obnoxious, on some level Anna truly cared about Becky.

She opened the refrigerator and smiled faintly. Becky was right. Everything she could possibly want or need for two days was there, even capers - a new unopened bottle of capers! Tears welled again in Anna's eyes.

"Chris, I think I'm falling apart," Anna had confided to Christopher Hayden, her closest colleague and good friend, the previous Wednesday.

"Anna, you are not falling apart, you have fallen," replied Chris. "I'll be down in twenty minutes, as soon as I get through this pile on my desk."

Normally, she would have ripped into him for such a remark, but not today, not this time. He was right, and she knew it. Wonderful, exasperating and competent Chris, her friend for more than twenty years, was management consultant and confidante to more than a few CEO's.

Anna and Chris had grown up together professionally, yet their connection went much deeper. She was the one who encouraged, if not shamed him first into leaving his coaching job at the local high school, and later into breaking away from his comfy executive VP spot at AT&T, to launch his now successful consulting firm. Chris was known nationally in corporate circles as "The Coach." He was the one who harassed her into writing her first book, *You Are Your Own Worst Enemy* and prodded her to do the second, *Get A Grip! Quit Whining, and Take Charge Of Your Life.* They had offices in the same building overlooking Flagler Drive, next door to Good Samaritan Hospital in West Palm Beach. The view from their windows was spectacular. The sparkling waters of the Intercoastal divided two worlds, with those who worked for a living on the mainland, looking over at those who lunched. Yachts, sailboats, pelicans and seagulls separated the strivers of the city from the rich in their mansions. Just up the street from their offices was the radio station where she broadcast her live show, "Get A Grip!" Anna had now hosted the popular call-in program for three years. It had been developed at Chris' urging, following the success of her book.

As she gazed at the tourists strolling along Flagler, Anna would marvel that she had stayed this long in South Florida. Had it really been twenty years since she moved here for a temporary fling? Now, to her chagrin, here she remained with not one, but two properties, one in West Palm, and a second up the coast in Vero Beach. Living in this tropical concoction of diverging cultures and values, Anna both loved and hated the area. She had taken a lot a grief for buying and remodeling that second property, until her friends saw the little house hidden from the road, sitting right along the Indian River. If the winding pathway lush with tropical foliage didn't create a spell, once inside the light and airy house, visitors were greeted with an expansive view of the water and its many inhabitants. This house became Anna's refuge - her sanctuary away from the world.

Anna's life was packed full; it was much more hectic and demanding than she cared to admit. She considered her time and space in the "river house," as it came to be called, almost sacred. Anna used time alone to recharge and center. She would meditate by the river, walk by the sea, talk aloud to the herons and sandpipers, and wave to the occasional dolphin or manatee that would cavort near her dock.

Beth, in particular, had loved the house and would join Anna there at least one weekend a year. It became a ritual after a while, one which they both treasured and coveted. They spent time talking and laughing, problem-solving and remembering. They shared the most intimate secrets about the joy and pain in their lives. They had political discussions as well as philosophical and metaphysical ones. There was nothing they couldn't and didn't discuss. One Sunday morning, Beth dragged Anna from her room to watch the space shuttle, *Endeavor*, take off. The two of them stood on the dock in the darkness of the early dawn, looking toward the skies. As the fiery ball of light soared toward the heavens, Beth and Anna turned their faces upward and together wished on this flying star. It was shortly after that visit that Beth was diagnosed with breast cancer. As she neared death, the two friends reminisced about that launch.

Beth's last refuge was Anna's river house. Beth died just as the sun rose on a beautiful South Florida morning that was filled with sunshine and tropical breezes. Her last hour was heralded by the sounds of birds chirping and the rippling waves of the river. It was as if all of nature acknowledged how special this woman was by coming together in a brilliant display of color and light to mark her passing.

Beth had wanted to die in an environment free of white uniforms and sterile rooms. Anna, of course, would have done anything to grant Beth's wishes and ease her suffering those last weeks. In a way, this was Anna's final gift to her dear friend. Tom and Beth's daughters managed to work around the space limitations. So Beth was able to live out those final days relatively pain-free, surrounded by the people who meant the most to her.

As Anna waited for Chris, she wrote a large check to the hospice and enclosed it in the letter she had written thanking the wonderful nurses who had taken such loving care of her friend. Chris walked into her inner office as she was sealing the envelope, sat down in one of the Windsor chairs, and favored her with his most penetrating gaze.

As usual, he got right to the point. "I've been waiting for your call, Annie, and not just since Beth's funeral," he said in that direct way of his. "I know you're in pain, and have been for some time. What can I do?"

Anna and Chris met regularly to hash out both business and personal problems. They would discuss each other's work over lunch or dinner, each benefitting from the other's complementary, yet very different perspective. She was the clinician. He was the jock who could translate her insights into a concise message which resonated with some of the most powerful players in corporate America. Their business understanding was based completely on trust. Not a penny ever exchanged hands. Their first venture at visible collaboration was the book they apprehensively had agreed to write the week before Beth died.

"This has best-seller written all over it," Anna's agent had exclaimed. "You've got a following that spans age and gender lines. And Chris is respected, if not revered, by the 'suits.' Together the two of you should pack quite a punch!"

Chris had been the reluctant one. "This could do it, Anna, we've never really had a disagreement worth talking about in all these years."

"So, what if we do lock horns, Chris?" Anna had replied, "We can weather it. Besides, I already know what an insufferable pain-in-the-butt you can be!"

And so was born the idea for Anna's third book and Chris' first, *Strategies For Success from The Coach & The Counselor*. And then Beth died.

Facing Chris in her office, she had needed a friend - someone to listen. Running her fingers through her hair, the annoying habit she could not rid herself of and a dead giveaway of careening emotions, Anna had taken off her glasses, making Chris a blur. "I don't know, Chris, I think I am really losing it. I feel so detached - like I'm just going through the motions. I feel like a hypocrite, especially with my clients, let alone when I'm on the air with callers," she had said. "I have this emptiness that just won't go away. I really don't know what I need or want, or what to do with my life. I have never felt so directionless."

He had frowned and in that confident, direct way of his had said, "Call Becky and get away for a few days, and then we'll decide what to do. Perhaps the Vineyard house is free some weekend soon. You know Becky and Michael won't be up there this time of year. Go away, collect your thoughts. See if you can get it together on your own. Annie, you have been through hell these past eighteen months. You have coped by filling your time with projects, people and work. It was bound to come to a halt at some point - this is it."

As he had turned to head for the door, Anna had thrown the small cross-stitch pillow made by one of her clients at the back of his head.

"I'm sorry about the book, Chris. We'll get started when I get back, okay?"

"Screw the book, Annie. I just wish I could make the hurt go away." He hadn't looked at her, and she understood this was the closest he could come to telling her how he felt.

She had immediately picked up the phone and called Becky in Connecticut.

A few days later, here she was. The mug was warm in her hands as she slowly sipped her tea, staring out at Lake Tashmoo. The whitecaps and rough water bounced the few remaining boats around like toys in a child's bath. It was late afternoon now, and the wind had picked up a bit. She unpacked her parka, felt in the pockets for her gloves, and headed out the door. The walk through the woods was blissfully quiet, and before long she was on the beach. Like a slap across her face, the cold, damp ocean wind instantly resurrected memories of the funeral. The ache in her chest resumed, and she felt tears sting her cheeks.

Anna pushed against the wind, making it out to the end of the jetty. "What is happening to me?" she whispered aloud. "I thought I had prepared myself for this." She recalled those final days and hours of Beth's life. She sobbed now as she had then with the knowledge that the inevitable had arrived.

Those hours and then minutes before death occurs always take too long. Then they are over too quickly. Anna had seen only one other person die, and that was her mother. The vigil that marked the end of that remarkable life had been very different than Beth's. Mother had died in the hospital, with activity all around. Most of the activity was contrived by the family and staff who, for very different reasons, attended to the unnecessary under the guise of making her mother "comfortable." Beth's passing was a tribute to Beth herself, who surrendered with a peace and dignity that bespoke her character. The nurses who cared for her and us, Anna reflected, lovingly created an environment of comfort and safety. Beth had left this life with all that mattered to her finished, and with those who meant the most in the world to her by her side. Anna watched and listened as the waves crashed up on the jetty rocks and began to feel better, though her sobs continued.

Suddenly aware of the setting sun and the water splashing up on the rocks, she shivered. Her knees and back stiff from the dampness, Anna started to get up. As she turned towards the beach, she saw a lone figure approaching several yards away, beckoning to her to wait. He carefully walked out toward her on the slippery rocks, hand extended. Puzzled, very stiff, and somewhat confused, she took his hand and followed him back to the sand.

"Are you okay?" he asked, letting go of her hand. "I was getting concerned about you. Look, the tide is coming in."

Now fully in the moment, Anna looked at the stranger, and recognized the man from the plane. "I'm fine, thanks. I just lost track of time."

Side by side they walked down the beach and through the woods, without saying another word.

4

Solitary Memories

They reached the back door to the house before she realized she had not introduced herself. At that moment the phone began to ring. "Forgive me, I'm Annie. Thanks for your offer of help both times today."

He looked at her kindly and seemed to want to say something, but Anna quickly opened the door and ran to pick up the phone before the answering machine retrieved the call.

"Thank goodness you answered this time. It is you, isn't it, Anna?"

Anna held the phone to one side for the duration of the monologue she knew would follow this greeting. It was from Becky, of course.

"Where have you been? I've called at least half a dozen times, and we were beginning to get worried. Anna? Anna, talk to me."

"I'm sorry, Becky, I meant to call and let you know that I was here, safe and generally sound. I've been out walking and just lost track of time. Patrick has taken care of everything, so I'm set for the weekend. You know you have the most reliable caretaker on the Vineyard."

Anna turned to invite the stranger in from the cold. But the door to the kitchen was closed, and the steps vacant.

"Well, just make yourself comfortable," Becky continued. "Michael and I want you to feel at home - what's ours is yours, dear Anna."

Please let this conversation end, Anna thought to herself. "I appreciate everything, Becky. Thanks again and don't worry about me. I'm a big girl, and I need to be here - alone. I will not be picking up the phone from now on, so please don't be alarmed. Leave me a message if you absolutely need to talk to me, okay?"

The receiver was practically in its cradle when Anna heard Becky's voice again.

"Anna, there is something else, I nearly forgot. The Duffy place. You know, look out the kitchen window to your left, through the trees. It's the A-frame in the distance. Mary called to let us know their house will be occupied this weekend, too, so don't be concerned if you see some activity down there."

"Okay, Becky, gotta go."

Anna sighed again, muttering to herself as she hung up the phone. "Great, that's all I need, some wild party tomorrow night, with middle-aged boomers flaunting their virility by streaking through the woods in thirty-degree weather after an afternoon of beer and football."

Still chilled, actually shaking with cold, she put on the kettle for a pot of tea, and went into the great room to light a fire. It was dark now, the house quite beautiful with the fading autumn shadows dancing over the Ralph Lauren and Waverly fabrics, throwing a peaceful silhouette on the room. Walking back to the kitchen, Anna's eyes misted as she reached for the Portmerion teapot.

It was as if she were squinting to see through heavy London

fog. As she held the white earthenware teapot sprinkled with flowers, bees and butterflies in a tremulous hand, Anna was transported across the great pond.

"I just love London," Beth exclaimed, as they emerged arm-in-arm from the Underground. They were headed in the direction of Harrods and Anna's favorite street, Beauchamp Place. They were on their way first to the off-price china shops, where Anna could browse and buy for hours. Anna loved a bargain, a trait for which she endured constant ribbing from Beth. Then off to Kensington to meander through the quaint and expensive, but not to be missed, shopping haunts of royals and rock stars.

"I'm glad I listened to you, Annie. Thanksgiving in London is just what I needed! What are you looking for today?" she asked, as they entered the first china shop.

"Portmerion," Anna replied with her trademark wink. "Help me search each corner - you never know when a piece with a discontinued pattern will jump right into your hands! I'll take the basement, and you can have the first floor."

That bittersweet trip had happened three years ago, but it seemed like yesterday. Anna had been away on a month-long project in Britain, promoting her first book, when she had received the card from Beth. It had taken close to a fortnight for the note to catch up with her, but Anna had smiled as she poured her tea and slit the top of the card.

Anna always looked forward to correspondence from her dearest friend. They had a ritual now, after these twenty years. They were lucky to get together two or three times a year, and it hadn't been even that frequent in the last five. With Anna's practice, media commitments, and book tours, and Beth's busy life juggling her law practice with raising two teenagers, and helping out with Tom's business, the two of them rarely got to see each other. So they had resorted to postcards whenever away, and notes on birthday cards to let each other know they were always in one another's thoughts. Occasionally they surprised each other with the unexpected card or letter, so Anna was anticipating a good laugh or at least a chuckle. Beth had a way with words. This was probably why she excelled as a lawyer, Anna would chide every time she had the chance.

The familiar Boston postmark told Anna there wasn't a move to announce, so she settled into a comfortable chair ready to have her spirits lifted. Taking her first sip of the hot, sweet tea, Anna was totally unprepared for what she began to read.

My dear Annie,

Forgive me for writing rather than calling, but I just couldn't bring myself to tell you this over the phone. I found out yesterday I have cancer. I had felt a lump in my breast earlier in the fall, and to make a long story short, had the biopsy last week and got the results yesterday. After much deliberation, I have scheduled surgery for after Thanksgiving. I'm still in shock, and very scared. I know this is a terrible way to ask you for help, but can you call me when you get a minute?

Please forgive me again for being such a coward about this. Thanx and I love you!

Beth

Anna's hand shook as she read and reread the card. What day was this? Has Thanksgiving come and gone? My God, what must Beth think? This was written two weeks ago, and she hasn't heard from me. With shaking hands, she pounded the numbers into the phone, staring at her watch and trying to calculate what time it was in the States as the phone began to ring. A groggy voice finally said hello.

"Beth, I'm in London, and I just opened your note. I'm so sorry it took all this time to find me. Are you awake? Are you okay?"

"Is that you, Annie? It's two o'clock in the morning here, and yes, I'm awake now. I'm so happy to hear from you," Beth said sleepily. Both of them started to cry.

Beth arrived at Gatwick two days later. Once Beth had settled into Anna's suite at the hotel, they took off for Kensington's slick cobblestone streets for an afternoon of shopping, during which Anna convinced Beth to help her find some bargains. Anna had purchased a collection of unique "finds" that day, one of which she now held in her hand. Anna had sent the Portmerion teapot to Becky for her forty-fifth birthday.

It had been damp and bitter cold that weekend in London, right before Beth's surgery. Just like today, Anna thought, as the whistling of the kettle startled her back to the present. The kitchen was totally dark now, except for the dial on the wall clock. Anna was surprised to see it was six o'clock.

"Maybe this wasn't such a good idea," she mumbled to herself, as the clinician in her assessed her state of mind. "I seem to be getting less focused, not more. Where has today gone?" Suddenly, she was very hungry and very tired.

The light from the refrigerator filled the room as she scanned the shelves for something to eat. Settling on Brie and grapes, she used the microwave to heat the cheese, and searched the cabinets for some crackers. Her plate of food prepared, she debated whether she dared have some wine. "I can't get any spacier than I already am," she said aloud, and opened the chilled chardonnay she saw hiding on the bottom shelf of the refrigerator.

Anna sat staring at the dying fire and poured herself a second glass of wine. Her hunger satisfied, and finally feeling warm for the first time since she'd arrived, she loaded the CD player with discs, pulled the afghan around her and curled up on the sofa to the sounds of classical music.

It was the silence that awakened her. Disoriented and somewhat apprehensive, she searched the room for anything familiar, slowly remembering where she was, and thinking it must be close to dawn. Once fully awake, the luminated hands of her watch confirmed that it was five o'clock. She noted the still full glass of wine, pulled herself up from the sofa, and took the wine bottle into the kitchen to re-cork it.

Anna was definitely not a morning person. So on the extremely rare occasions when she found herself actually awake before seven o'clock, she got moving. With a pot of coffee brewing, she took a long, very hot shower, marveling at how she was actually preparing for a Saturday at five-fifteen in the morning. With dawn an hour away, Anna headed out for a drive.

Logically, one would go down-island to watch the sunrise. But Anna found herself driving in the direction of Gay Head, the extreme westernmost end of the island. It was a special place that Anna found mystical, even sacred in its remote beauty. A thermos of coffee by her side and the Explorer starting to warm up, Anna almost smiled as she tackled the winding road up-island. It was misty and quite foggy, and before long Anna found herself encased in a cloud. She saw the cemetery on her right and pulled down the gravel road almost by instinct.

Leaving the fog lights on, she got out of the car, and walked up the slight incline and inside the fence. "I haven't been to John Belushi's grave in years," she said to no one. But what a fitting place to wait for the fog to pass. Sitting on the slate bench facing his name, she looked down at the gravemarker, smiling at the collection of beer and wine bottles flanking his name. Pouring herself a cup of coffee, flashes of the brilliant and tragic comic and his companions in those now famous television skits danced before her eyes.

"Annie, we shouldn't be eating strawberry shortcake this late at night," Beth had exclaimed as she piled a generous helping of ice cream and strawberries over the just baked shortcake.

"Oh, will you relax?" Anna retorted. "We'll laugh off all those calories. Hurry up! Saturday Night Live just started. Besides, we walked all over the North End today, fought our way through Filene's basement, and practically ran down Boylstown Street from Copley to Kenmore Square. You're worried about a few calories?"

After graduating from the University of Maryland, they had ended up in Boston. Eventually, they both attended Boston University, with Anna studying psychology and Beth, law. Saturday Night Live started out as a filler for those dateless Saturday nights and grew to become their favorite way to end the week. Before long, they had an apartment full of people every Saturday night, with their own cast of characters and wannabees, almost as funny as Chevy and Bill, John and Dan, Jane and Gilda. Back then, the silliness and satire created a perfect backdrop to the transition to adulthood challenging Anna and her friends. Anna would see patients all week, and be grilled each Friday morning by her supervising psychologist as to approach and intervention. Beth would spend hours in the law library each morning before she was off to the Legal Aid clinic in

Boston's South End. Anna would leave Boston City Hospital, meet up with Beth, and they would hop the MBTA back to Commonwealth Avenue. It was on one of those Saturday nights during the sparring between Jane and Gilda as they reported on the "news" of the day, that Tom and Beth announced their engagement. They were married the week after Beth sat for the bar exam, and within three years had produced two beautiful baby girls. Even then, every Saturday night, either Anna or Beth would call the other as the guest host of the week appeared on the screen. That ritual abruptly ended the week John Belushi died. It was as if someone had pulled the plug on their escape route. Yet as the cancer ate away at her friend's spirit, Anna had sent Beth a whole set of Saturday Night Live tapes from the early years, knowing that laughter was good for the soul.

The fog was lifting slightly. Anna thought she heard a rustle and some footsteps. A brief but intense fear spread through her, until she realized she was on Martha's Vineyard and not in South Florida. She turned to see the stranger for the third time now, and realized it was tears, not fog, blurring her vision.

5

Lost in a Sea of Pain

h e had given her quite a start. Could he have heard her talking to the wind?

The rain started softly as Anna stared at the stranger. This was now their third encounter, making her feel very uncomfortable and unusually vulnerable. Was he following her? Her guard was not totally down. After all, Anna lived in South Florida where, as anyone knows, suspicion and being on alert is paradoxically a way of life in that tropical paradise. Who is this man? Why is he here? How should she handle this? Conflicting thoughts clouded her consciousness, and then she began to feel angry. Anna stood up abruptly and looked directly at him, when it suddenly came to her. Visibly, she relaxed. Of course. This man is the guest of the Duffy's - the person staying at the house next door, whom Becky had mentioned.

She smiled tentatively. "You show up at the most interesting times, and in the most unexpected places. We'll both catch our death," flinching as she uttered the word, "of cold if we stay here any longer." Suddenly hungry, she blurted, "Would you care to join me for breakfast?"

He strapped his bike on the top of the Explorer and together they headed east, this time away from the fog and into the rain.

Unaccountably, especially for a person as circumspect and private as she, Anna found herself talking to him about Beth's death. As they approached the Edgartown-Vineyard Haven Road, Anna realized she was monopolizing the conversation. Neither apologetic nor self-conscious, Anna was aware she was talking nearly non-stop about herself to this total stranger. Dr. Anna Carroll, usually the one listening, began to tell this man her life story, and as her story took life, she listened to herself perhaps for the very first time.

It was as though once released, her innermost feelings flowed out from her soul. She marveled as she heard herself disclose to this stranger buried fears about her own brush with cancer. The odd part was that the more she spoke, the more she wanted to reveal. Instead of being sated, she felt compelled, indeed urged on to greater and more profound depths of disclosure and release. It was as if she were making up for lost time.

Was it the somber atmosphere of the island this rainy day? Was it his gentle nature? His eyes conveyed acceptance and understanding, devoid of judgment and opinion. Something about him gave her comfort. There was something familiar and reassuring about his eyes.

Was it that Anna was so exhausted, she didn't care how she sounded? Was she so alone that she would tell this stranger about her secrets and her pain? Sitting in a deserted cafe on Water Street, looking through the sea sprayed mist clouding the irregular seventeenth century panes of glass, she began weeping softly about the baby.

"Beth was the only one who knew. All these years, she was the only one who knew the story. Kevin and I were in college. He was a senior and I was a year behind. We met, ironically, at an anti-war rally during the spring semester, 1968. It was my first, and to be honest, I was really there more out of curiosity than protest.

"The attraction was immediate and intense. It was as if from the moment our eyes met, we were joined together in a cosmic, karmic embrace. From the minute I met him, we were inseparable. Kevin and I spent every waking minute together for close to four months. I have never had another relationship like it. I have never felt that level of intensity nor experienced such passion or connection again in my life.

"Kevin had been accepted to law school and had great aspirations of going into politics and reforming the world. We all did back then, though he unquestionably would have become someone who could make a difference. He ended up going to Vietnam instead of Yale. Kevin was killed during the Tet Offensive along with countless others - the friends, lovers, husbands, brothers, sons and fathers - who died before their time.

Anna realized she had choked on the word "fathers"; she had never connected Kevin to fatherhood until that moment. But then, she hadn't talked about this for at least twenty-five years.

"Kevin had been in Vietnam only ten days before he was killed. He had left two weeks before for the west coast. He never even got to read the first and last letter I wrote him just after he left. I found out I was pregnant in the morning and that Kevin had been killed that afternoon. We were taking classes that summer. Beth heard me vomiting in the dorm bathroom.

" 'Annie, how far along are you?' she asked.

"I looked at her and said, 'When did Kevin leave for 'Nam?' and threw up again in the cold white bowl.

"I went for a walk in the early afternoon and found myself in front of the Catholic church on the main street of town. It was

Saturday, and afternoon confessions had just started. I was pulled inside, desperate for consolation, understanding, maybe even advice. I must have sat there for two hours, because confessions ended at four o'clock, and I was the last one to enter the little cubicle.

"As I started, the words, then tears came, and I just blurted out, 'Father, I think I'm pregnant. My boyfriend is in Vietnam, and I still have two years of school to finish. I don't know what to do.'

"He interrupted me at that point and said something like, 'So you aren't married, my dear?' I shook my head and started to answer, but without waiting for my reply, he began, 'You know you have committed a terrible sin. You have had sex outside of the sacrament of marriage. You have disappointed God, your parents, the Church. You know this is a terrible sin.'

"I swear he didn't even hear me get up and leave the confessional. I could still hear him lecturing me, the voice rising in pitch as the big oak doors slammed shut. It was a very long time, a decade or more, before I would even enter a church, and that was the last time I ever stepped foot into a confessional.

"I stormed back to my room, feeling very defiant and strong just then, the episode in the church energizing me in an odd sort of way. Beth greeted me, with grave concern in her eyes. I tried to reassure her. 'Beth,' I said, 'it's not that bad. Everything will be all right, you'll see.'

"She seemed tense, and I was actually thinking that maybe I shouldn't have involved her. She was a very sensitive person, and I was feeling guilty that I had unburdened on her.

" 'Annie, sit down,' she said grimly. 'This letter just came for you. It looks like it's from Kevin's mother.'

"I sat on my bed, looked into her face, and went pale. Her hands trembled as she handed me the letter. I stared at the return address and remember feeling a sudden rush of nausea. My hands shook and my heart started to beat wildly. I handed the envelope back to Beth and asked her to read what I already knew to be inside. As Beth tried to choke out the words that Kevin's mother had written to me, key phrases like 'he was very brave' and 'he died serving his country' assaulted my ears. I grabbed the letter from her hands and read it over and over until I fell into a fitful sleep.

"Sometime later, I remember being awakened from a terrible nightmare of blood and screams. Kevin was standing beside my bed, his hand on my face saying, 'I'm so sorry, Annie, this isn't the way it was supposed to be.' I was the one screaming, and it was Beth's hand on my face, not Kevin's. She was crying and trying to console me. We sat there like two little girls holding each other tight, crying and rocking back and forth on the bed. 'This time it's my turn to take care of you, Annie. I'll always be here for you. Don't worry, you will always have me.' "

Anna sighed deeply. She gazed listlessly at the gray rain streaming down the windows and felt as desolate as the view from her booth. Her shoulders sagging from emotional exhaustion, Anna paused, took a deep breath and tried to find the courage to continue with her story.

"Beth's mother had died when she was fifteen. We were inseparable, as we had been all through grammar school. Her mother had breast cancer and died the summer before we entered our junior year. One night after her mother's funeral, I stayed over at Beth's house. She had a wonderful canopy bed, with a wedding-veil like covering. We stayed up the whole night talking. We lay there hand in hand, and Beth told me about the day her mother died. I remember that night very clearly. Beth didn't cry at all. She just held my hand and told me how scared she was, how quiet and lonely her house was now that it was just her and her dad. She made me promise that I would never die and go away and leave her like her mother did. 'Of course, I won't ever leave you, Beth. We are friends forever. I'll never go away, even if you want me to.' Now in our junior year in college, she was consoling me."

Garish images pounded against Anna's skull. She remembered how the next morning after the worst night of her life, the nightmare continued. She went into the bathroom, feeling the wetness on her thighs. Stunned, she stared as the blood dropped in rivulets of red. The droplets turned into tissue and then into crimson rivers. Anna groaned now as she had groaned then, watching what was left of Kevin ebb away. Just how many lives were lost that day so long ago?

She was oblivious to the stranger now, lost in a sea of pain, as she continued.

"Beth found me on the bathroom floor still bleeding, curled in a fetal position, with the letter crumpled in my hand. The pregnancy was gone as quickly as it had come, terminated by either my shock at the news of Kevin's death, or my rage at the priest. Perhaps both.

"Beth is the only one who knew I was pregnant and lost my baby," Anna said. "She alone knew how hard I've worked all these years to plug the hole in my heart. Beth is the only one who knows about my life that was not to be.

" 'I'll tell Kevin about the baby for you, Annie, when I'm on the other side,' she said in those final hours. 'And remember, I'll always be here for you.'

"Beth died just three hours later," Anna said, concluding her story.

Tears streaming down her cheeks, Anna looked up into the gentle eyes of the man sitting across the table from her. His gaze was steady and deep, and tears matching hers fell from his eyes. He reached across the table, put his hand on top of hers, and turned his head toward Edgartown Harbor.

6

The Beckoning Light

*1*t was nine o'clock now, and the rain showed no signs of stopping. It was going to be a miserably bleak, depressing day. But Anna didn't feel depressed at all. She felt very strange. Tired, but at the same time energized. She had never told anyone that story, ever. She looked across the table at his face and again was amazed at how comfortable she felt. There was something remotely familiar about him, yet she was sure they had never met. Anna was just about to ask him if they had, when he looked away from her in the direction of the little island of Chappaquiddick.

"Are you up for a walk by the ocean, Annie? This weather will break, I just feel it. You have the perfect vehicle for exploring the dunes. Let's go see what answers Cape Pogue has to offer today."

And with that, he stood up and walked towards the Explorer.

Anna loved the wildlife refuge, but thought even the few birds and animals remaining would be wise enough to keep shelter on a drenchingly wet day like this. She silently followed him out the door anyway, got behind the wheel, and drove the

Explorer onto the barge that would take them across the harbor and deposit them on Chappaquiddick.

The barge, endearingly referred to as the "on-time ferry," had no schedule. It carried people and vehicles across the inlet upon demand. Once she settled her vehicle on the barge, Anna couldn't take her eyes off the light that beckoned from the Edgartown lighthouse. She was hypnotized by flashes of light that danced across the windshield in an even, predictable rhythm. As she stared at the beam, Anna thought she heard someone call her name. She turned very suddenly. The bright light grew before her eyes momentarily blinding her, so all she could do was listen.

"You are fine, Anna," said the reassuring nurse. "The surgery went well. You are fine."

The pain was unlike any she had ever experienced. And just as she became aware of the pain, the first wave of nausea consumed her. Lips chattering, she stammered, "I feel awful."

"You are in the recovery room, Dr. Carroll." It was a male voice now. "I'm going to give you something for the pain. You are doing fine."

She remembered thinking they must mean that there was no cancer. That's what they mean by fine, she had thought, because I'm not fine, I feel awful. But all she had said was thank you as she felt the pain medication course through her veins.

"Annie, Annie," the voice startled her, "you can start the engine now."

They drove the brief distance from the ferry toward the Cape. As they passed the Japanese gardens, the rain began to let up. The dunes were almost in sight now. Anna pulled the Explorer close to the marker describing the wildlife that inhabited the preserve. Only four-wheel drive vehicles were allowed out on the dunes, and permits were required at that.

While Anna was sure Becky and Michael would have followed the rules, she was inclined to overlook them. But driving the dunes on this bleak day seemed like trespassing, so she turned to her companion and said, "Let's walk out to the Cape. Nature seems too pensive today to be disturbed."

The trek over the infamous footbridge to East Beach always gave Anna a start, and today was no different. She felt a chill run through her as she thought about the young woman who died that awful night and the media swarm that followed. And for the first time, Anna realized she had also lost Kevin and her baby in July so long ago. A deep melancholy enveloped her. She was oblivious to her companion's help up the mound of soft, wet sand which gave the Cape its allure and challenge.

The view once over the slight crest was breathtaking, rain or not. In fact, Anna noticed that it had almost stopped. Only miles of sand and water were between them and the other side of the world. As she turned to speak to him, she saw he had started walking up the beach. Hurrying to reach him, she nearly tripped in the deep sand. He turned, as if he had heard her behind him, and patiently waited for her to catch up.

They proceeded side by side down the long, deserted beach. The stranger with the deep soulful eyes looked at Anna and asked, "What is it about your friendship with Beth that is making you so sad, Anna?"

Anna felt her cheeks flush with anger. "Because she's dead, that's why I'm sad. How can you ask such an obvious question?!"

"Ah, but Annie," he continued, seemingly oblivious to her anger, "You just told me the last words Beth spoke before she died were, 'I'll always be here for you.' You loved and trusted your friend, didn't you, Annie? Beth O'Neill wouldn't make a promise like that if she didn't intend to keep it."

Startled by his bluntness, Anna almost turned and walked away. But she looked over at him and those kind eyes kept her right on the path they had started. She looked down at the tracks she was making in the sand. That's funny, she thought, I don't remember mentioning Beth's last name.

His words sunk in. Anna considered what he had said and had to admit he had a point. She had never really listened to her dying friend's last words.

"You know," Anna began, "maybe you're right. My sadness has more to do with me than our friendship or Beth. I have had so many losses these past two years that I just gave into the emptiness when Beth died. Maybe this feeling has very little to do with death and loss. Maybe it's really about fear and change."

The two of them stopped and sat on the dune. Anna began digging with her heels, making deep crevices in the sand, and continued to speak.

"All my connections have shifted, much like the sands under our feet. Nothing seems to be permanent anymore, though that sounds ridiculous even as I say the words. Nothing has ever been permanent, but somehow it's different now. I suppose I need to see the loss as just a transition - Beth is still here and still my friend, just in a different form. I need to learn how to rework the connection so the relationship can continue."

"Beth will always be a real and permanent part of your life, Annie," he said, "if you will allow yourself to let the old way of connecting fade away, and open your heart so you can see her as she is now."

Anna looked over at him and wondered if she understood.

They stood up and together walked to the tip of the Cape. They sat down again on the sand and silently gazed out into the horizon. The rain had stopped, and there was some promise of sun. As she turned to tell him he'd been right, they would have sun after all, she caught a blurred glimpse of him fading out of sight on his way down the beach.

7

Waves of Memories

Anna walked slowly, in a deliberate sort of way, back toward the dunes. The sun was fully out now, shining uncharacteristically brightly for November. What a strange turn in the weather, she thought, as she lifted her face to bask in its rays. While it was not any warmer, Anna felt perfectly comfortable as she unzipped her jacket and faced the forceful, yet soothing waves of the Atlantic Ocean.

Anna closed her eyes, drawing the misting sea air deep within her lungs. Over the screech of the gulls, Anna heard her grandmother's voice.

"Annie, Annie, be careful! Don't get too much sun!" her grandmother had warned her over the sound of crashing waves. "Come here and at least put a cover and hat on. I know it's not hot out, but the sun will burn your fair skin." Anna ran to her beloved grandmother but fidgeted, anxious to get back to the water's edge and resume playing in the waves.

It was early summer. Anna, her parents, and her grandmother had driven down to Ocean City, Maryland. They were staying in a hotel right on the boardwalk. During the chilly nights, Anna would walk hand in hand between her grandmother and mother, fascinated by the noisy arcades with games of chance. They browsed the bright stores filled with endless glitter and enjoyed the delicious smells of peanuts and cotton candy, salt water taffy and macaroons. The little girl never toddled far from her grandmother and when she returned, she was quickly gathered into those familiar, soft, and so reassuring arms and walked briskly back to the hotel room.

Anna smiled at her grandmother and declared, "I'm okay, Grandma. I'm a BIG girl now and you don't have to worry about me anymore." The little girl loved her grandmother more than words could say.

"So much love for such a little girl," her grandmother would remark, as she gathered her into her large bosom, smelling of talcum powder and perfume.

Anna remembered how her mother would put lemon juice in her hair and rub ointment on her shoulders as she ran back and forth to the water's edge, filling her orange pail with water to fill the hole she and her father had dug in the sand. Sometimes, in later years, when there were more children, Anna's father and mother would drive the family down to the shore just for the day during the summer. Anna never knew until much later it was because they couldn't afford to stay in a hotel during the peak season. She believed her parents when they told her that the best time to go to the beach was when the crowds were sparse, and that's why they went to the shore in early June or September.

Anna hated having to put her shoes on over her wet and sandy feet to make the trek over the scalding sand to the car. Her mother would carry her brother and she would have to walk. She really didn't think it was fair, but her mother told her that's what growing up was all about.

"I should have asked her before she died what she meant

by that," Anna mumbled aloud. "Was it that growing up meant walking unassisted, or did she want me to get used to those irritating grains of sand in my shoes?"

Those early years, Anna was convinced, solidified her character. She knew she had been blessed even before she could speak in sentences and knew, even during the later, more difficult times that she was indeed lucky to have been born to such fine people. Anna was the oldest of six children, each as different as they were similar. Anna was the first, not only of her clan, but of twelve grandchildren counting both sides. For almost four years, the little girl was an only child of doting parents, two sets of bickering grandparents, a slew of strange, but equally doting aunts, uncles, great and grand aunts, and some distant cousins often talked about, but rarely if ever seen.

These are the most critical years of development, she would later learn as she sailed through her psychology classes, thinking that most of what her professors took three hours a week to cover was simply common sense. As she listened hour after hour, day after day, year after year, to the horrors experienced by those troubled souls who sought her counsel, Anna grew even more grateful for her early years. Not that they were perfect by any stretch, but her family ills and quirks paled in comparison to the stories that filled her office. She knew that her blessed upbringing was just preparation for her life's work, and that in a strange, almost karmic way she would be able to help people feel better about themselves, and their lives, if only they would listen.

Listening is in essence the job of a psychologist. Of course, it is much more than that. But if the truth were really to be told, Anna was convinced that if children had parents who really listened to them, there would be a lot of unemployed psychologists. Her colleagues were appalled when she came out with blunt simplifications like that, and virtually ostracized her as her message gained popularity and credibility. Initially, Anna was quite disturbed about all the uproar until Beth and Chris pointed out that she had never cared what people said or thought about her, and that's what made her so refreshing to be around. So, Anna ventured even further out on a limb and said that the ability to listen and to love were the hallmarks of a well-functioning adult, and that everything else was just window dressing. While not rocket science, Anna knew these abilities were harder to practice than any exercise regimen.

Maybe that's why Beth meant so much to me, she considered, as the waves touched the tips of her sneakers. As time went on, Beth was the only one who really listened to me. Maybe she was the only one all these years I've allowed in my heart.

Anna could taste the salt in the air as the wind whipped her hair back from her face. As she looked down, a foaming wave crested over her feet, soaking them. The bitter cold of the sea shocked her into awareness.

Now she was uncomfortable, her feet clammy and cold. "I hate wet, sandy feet," she mumbled and began sloshing toward the Explorer.

As the sand gave under her feet, Anna was distracted by yet another familiar voice. She stumbled down the dunes, then slid, not watching her footing because she was concentrating on listening. Losing her balance, she fell backward. In frustration and resignation, she sat in the very wet sand. Anna was stunned to hear a stern yet comforting voice call to her over the dunes.

"Annie Carroll and Beth O'Neill, get in here this very minute. You two girls will not be getting any sympathy from me or anyone else if you get sick and miss your Christmas play," Anna's mother had scolded.

She was a solid, consistent and very Irish woman who

demonstrated little if any affection openly, except when it came to Beth. Anna remembered how her mother had embraced Beth after her own mother died, pulling her in as one of the family. She was able to show Beth a tenderness she withheld from her own offspring. Anna never minded. Even though her mother's way of caring was to scold or criticize, and, though it took Anna some years to figure this out, once she did, she relaxed and generally overlooked mother's abrasiveness. This time, however, was different.

She was very angry at her mother and, in typical twelve year old fashion, turned to Beth and said, "Just ignore her. She'll forget about us in a minute or two, once we are out of sight. Let's go make angels in the snow." And so they did.

Anna and Beth, both soaked to the bone, walked the two miles to the public school playground (it was much bigger than the Catholic school's), and made the best angels ever, until their arms ached and their lips turned blue.

"Look, Annie," Beth said, "I'll bet we've made at least fifty different ones now. Let's go pick out our guardian angels."

By the time they had carefully sorted through the figures they had created and decided which each would claim for her own, it was dark, very cold, and both girls were close to being frostbitten. And while these two less-than-angelic girls did miss out on their Christmas play, they had no regrets. The playing they did together was much more fun than any old costume pageant. Anna's mother, while not sympathetic, propped her up in the big double bed, put on the vaporizer, and had her brother and sister bring her cups of tea. She even got to watch her favorite TV show, over protests from her siblings, of course, because it wasn't her turn.

Anna laughed out loud as she got up and started again down the dune. But not before she made a very big and very beautiful angel in the wet sand.

"Please watch over Beth up there," Anna whispered to the figure she had just created. "She's new to heaven and could use a friend." With that Anna hopped in the Explorer, drove to the ferry landing, and drifted across the harbor to the other side.

Anna looked at her watch, surprised to see that it was one o'clock. She had taken off her shoes and socks and put the heater on full blast, directed toward the floor of the Explorer. By the time she drove off the ferry, her feet were dry. The shoes and socks, however, were another story. So she drove back to Tisbury by way of the Beach Road, her bare feet working the accelerator and brake. Smiling to herself, she turned the Explorer toward Oak Bluffs, picturing Beth laughing and her mother shaking her head in disapproval. She wondered if these kindred spirits had found each other yet.

Oak Bluffs, the funky summer town of the island, is bordered by a picture postcard array of gingerbread houses built by Methodists at the turn of the century. Anna loved the place. With their pastel colors and decorative trimwork, the houses reminded her of childhood fantasies. The town itself held memories of those wild and reckless times from which everyone needed to escape in the late sixties and early seventies. It is a somewhat inconsistent place, a mixture of illusion and decadence, nightclubs and revival pavilions, populated by newly-rich celebrities dressed like bums and bums living off million dollar trusts, believing they were celebrities.

She saw him almost the minute she made the turn into Oak Bluffs. Strange she should recognize his back. But she just knew it was him. Honking the horn, she slowed down and pulled toward the curb. He looked up, stopped the bike and smiled.

"How about a lift, stranger?" Anna called, suddenly aware she had not yet asked his name.

"Where did you get to, Annie? I looked for you but there was no sight of either you or the Explorer, so I just headed off to see the rest of the island, and was lucky to see the ferry pull up."

He looks different, Anna thought, barely hearing his question.

"Annie, Annie, Hellooo!!! Why are you in bare feet? It is the middle of November, not June, you know!"

Startled, Anna looked down at her feet and laughed, realizing for the first time how cold they were. Smiling, she told him about her mother and grandmother and the angels in the snow.

8

Turbulent Soul

Anna stared out at the clear skies and rough ocean as he strapped the bike to the roof of the Explorer. Only dimly aware of the activity around her, Anna listened to the waves break against the seawall.

A powerful wave of memory crashed into her consciousness as the sea water foamed and frothed against the wall. Anna distinctly heard Beth's plea, even over the churning waters of a turbulent ocean.

"Annie, I don't think I can continue much farther," Beth said, as she pulled the bike off to the side of the road. "Let's rest a minute, please."

Anna looked at her pale and winded friend. Promptly, she parked her bike as well, and hailed down the first pickup that came along. It had been an ambitious plan, Anna had thought from the beginning, but Beth was insistent. Anna had gone along, despite her misgivings, thinking who was she to deny her friend anything? They had rented the bikes in Vineyard Haven, and had made it through the hilly part of the trip, past the carousel. The faint sounds of accordion music wafted from the oldest carousel in the country and drifted past them as they had struggled to make it up the incline. They were almost to the easy part of the trip, the turn in the road to essentially flat terrain. As they passed by the hotel on the hill, Beth had called to her. She was weak and shaky, but once they got a lift back to the house, her color had improved, and her breathing had returned to normal.

Anna was fixing hot chocolate when she heard Beth pull out one of the kitchen chairs.

"Sit down, please, Ann," she said, her voice flat and unusually firm. Anna couldn't remember a time when she had called her by just Ann.

"What is it, Beth? What's the matter?" Anna sat directly across from her, looking into those blue eyes that suddenly seemed very far away.

"I'm not going to make it, am I?" Beth asked abruptly. Anna just looked at her. "Don't bullshit me, Annie. Tell me what you honestly think."

Beth rarely used profanity, so that, coupled with her tone of voice took Anna off guard. She was speechless and then became very uncomfortable. Anna put her head in her hands and began to run her fingers through her hair.

"Beth, I don't know how to answer such a question. How do I know what your chances are? I'm living each day believing you will make it. I haven't allowed myself to seriously consider any alternative. And that's the truth."

"Well, start considering it," Beth said in a firm, flat voice. "I want to talk about the alternative, because I don't think I can fight this any longer, and I need to talk it through with somebody. I don't want you to pull any professional crap on me, okay? I just want you to tell me honestly about what you think and feel in your heart. You've always had a sixth sense about things, Annie, and I know you've got a feeling about what's happening here too."

Anna sighed and pushed the chair away from the table. Since this last round of chemo, and after seeing how Beth looked as they sat huddled on the deck of the ferry on their way to the island, Anna knew her best friend was going to die. She knew death was imminent as clearly as she had seen the lighthouse blinking on their left as they had pulled out of Woods Hole into the Sound. She knew Beth was dying, and she had known they would have this conversation at some point during their trip. Still, she hadn't expected it now.

"Okay, Beth. Let's talk about it," she said softly. Taking her friend's hands into her own, Anna said, "I'm not in control here, Beth. You are. This is your life, not mine."

Beth began to cry and pulled her hands from Anna's. She pushed her chair away from the table and went over to the window. Her back facing Anna, she again asked, "So, what do you think, Annie? Am I going to die?"

Anna got up from the table and went over to her friend. She turned her around so that the two faced each other. Anna put her hands squarely on Beth's shoulders and said, "Yes, Beth, you are going to die. So am I. So, what's new here, huh? You are not going to leave until you decide it's time. You are in control of that."

"Do you think I have much longer, Annie?"

"You have as long as you need, Beth. So let's talk about what you have left to do."

It was either the door opening or his voice that brought her back. "So, what do you have left to do today, Annie?" he asked as he climbed into the Explorer.

Somewhat startled, Anna looked at him, and said, "For right now, how about something and someplace warm?" And with that, she scanned the rear view mirror for cars or bikes before pulling back onto the road.

As they drove past the pavilion on the green, the sun glistened off the windows of the pink gingerbread house. Anna had to shield her eyes to cut the glare.

"These houses are amazing," she heard him say. "Do people actually live in them?"

"Only in the summer," Anna responded, "They aren't winterized. The pink house is my favorite," she said, pointing to her left.

Anna stopped the Explorer abruptly and stared as if caught by the spell cast from Victorian house. Over crashing waves, she could faintly hear a familiar, high-pitched childish voice call to her.

"Pink is my favorite color, Annie, so at least one bedroom and one bathroom must be pink."

"Okay, Beth, but I want a white bathroom and a blue kitchen. And I want to put wallpaper in the living and dining rooms."

It was the summer they were eleven years old. Anna's father had finally finished the long awaited dollhouse. Both girls were delirious with excitement. They had collected piles of fabric scraps and magazines, leftover paint, and shoeboxes full of every discarded thing you could think of to use in the interior design. It was to go in Anna's room, but for now it sat on her father's workbench in the cool, musty cellar. They worked on it every day for the entire summer, and by the time it was finished, it was magnificent. Even Anna's mother was impressed. "Well," she said, "you two girls should be decorators. Now which of you will keep it clean?"

The two girls giggled and took pictures of the pink gingerbread house with Beth's Brownie camera. They had Anna's father take a picture with each of them on either side of the structure. Even though it was a black and white picture, Anna never forgot how pink it was.

But they never did play with it. That was the last summer they played with dolls or amused themselves with such frivolous activities. Beth's mother was diagnosed with breast cancer two weeks after school started that September, and the cancer changed everything.

"Cancer changes everything," Anna heard herself say as the pink house faded from sight. She looked over at her passenger and saw that he was staring out to sea. Anna looked straight ahead unsure if she had spoken aloud or to herself. Before she knew it, they were pulling into Vineyard Haven, the legendary tavern seeming to beckon to them.

9

A Familiar Friend

Anna put her shoes on the hearth to dry while lunch was served. The fire warmed the room, and Anna was glad they were the only patrons in the place. It was usually bustling with tourists, so much so that, unless you were a first-time "day-tripper," as the locals called the people who flocked over each day from Falmouth, no one would dare attempt to lunch at the famous harborside restaurant on a Saturday during the summer months. But this wasn't the summer, and she welcomed the emptiness she knew they would find. She couldn't remember when she had tasted chowder this good. Looking out over the harbor, she watched as the ferry left the dock.

"I remember the last time I was on that ferry," she said as she looked across the table into those now familiar eyes. "Beth and I spent a week here a year before the cancer prevailed. I think it was one of the most significant experiences in my life."

"Tell me about it, Annie," he said gently. So, she again started talking to him about herself.

"I've been flooded with memories ever since I arrived on the island yesterday," she began, "strange and very disconnected flashes of my life up until Beth's funeral. On the drive here to the tavern, I got swallowed up in my memories of the pink doll-house Beth and I decorated when I pointed out the gingerbread cottages to you in Oak Bluffs. Then back on Cape Pogue, after you took off down the beach, I had such vivid memories of my grandmother and mother when I was very young that I actually made an angel in the snow, I mean sand, for Beth. Then, as we were driving along Beach Road, I remembered that last week here and the conversations we had about death. Beth changed after our 'Vineyard Retreat,' as she referred to it; she seemed physically weaker, but emotionally and spiritually stronger."

"How do you feel now, Anna?"

She thought it odd how he switched from calling her Annie to Anna, but she answered him anyway.

"Better than I did this morning sitting on that cold rock in the graveyard, that's for sure!" she replied. Anna collected her now dry footwear from the hearth, dressed her feet, paid the bill, waved to him and hopped in the Explorer to go back to the house. "See you later," she called to him as she eased out onto the road. Suddenly she remembered his bike and abruptly pulled over. Leaping out, Anna contemplated the now-vacant roof of the Explorer. She was puzzled, having no recollection of him unstrapping the bicycle.

Sighing aloud, Anna hopped back into the driver's seat and headed into Vineyard Haven proper. Her destination was one of the best bookstores anywhere, snuggled in between the T-shirt shops that line winding Main Street. The bookstore is a wonderful place to browse, and get lost, especially up on the second floor. They had gone there together, she and Beth, and spent hours perusing nutrition and holistic healing books. Today I am going to go where the spirit takes me, Anna thought.

"What a positive omen!" Anna said aloud, as the space

directly in front of the bookstore opened up. The thirty-something young man in a battered pick-up tipped his cap as he left the space just for her. There's just something about the folks who live here, Anna thought, as she smiled and waved back at the young man, or is it that life here is just so different from south Florida?

Anna went directly to the upper floor, making a mental note to pick up a paper before she left. She needed to check Sunday's tide schedule so she could plan her trip out to the rocky beach at Gay Head. As she walked past the children's section, she caught a glimpse of a floppy denim hat with big yellow sunflowers decorating the brim. She could just make out a small freckled face framed with red curls staring back at her with a puzzled expression. Anna's heart skipped a beat.

Anna blinked and rubbed her eyes. It was as if the bee perched on the middle flower had jumped over to her shoulder and begun humming in her ear. Anna again clearly heard Beth's voice.

"I'm going to do it, Annie, and you're going to help me," Beth had said as she pulled the large-brimmed denim hat from the shopping bag. "This hair, what's left of it, has got to go."

So Anna and Beth had gone upstairs to the bathroom, where they first cut, then very carefully shaved Beth's hair. The chemo had left Beth with patchy tufts of the once shiny, copper-penny hair she'd always been so proud of. It had been Beth's idea to use Michael's electric razor, and they giggled like schoolgirls about how they'd put one over on him.

"He is so damned fastidious." Beth exclaimed. "The man presses his underwear!"

The event turned into a party, and since Beth felt well enough to have some wine, they toasted each other with a very expensive merlot. Anna applied vivid tattoos of flowers, hearts, butterflies, and bees she'd bought for her nieces all over Beth's head. The next day, Beth, outfitted in her new denim hat and sporting fading tattoos, went into Edgartown with Anna, where they bought two baseball caps. One was a very feminine cap a la Laura Ashley, the other a shiny yellow metallic with a visor. They stopped next in Oak Bluffs and bought the last straw hat and several more baseball and golf caps in the only store still open that late in October. All told, Beth left the island with six hats, but her favorite was the floppy denim.

Her eyes riveted on the sunflowers, Anna was momentarily unaware of a steady tugging at her sleeve.

"Excuse me, lady, but can you help me find a book on bees?"

The spell broken, Anna looked down as the child's denim hat slipped off her head and toppled onto the floor. They both stooped to retrieve it. Anna remained on her knees in order to connect at the child's level. As she peered at freckles so close she could count them, Anna felt a lump in her throat.

"This is my favorite hat," declared the little voice, as the child brushed some dust from the brim. "My mom says it is a summer hat and I shouldn't be wearing it now. But today's my birthday, so I'm allowed. I need to find a book about bees," she continued. "Do you know if bees understand English? Joey, he's my brother, says bees will attack my hat next summer. I need to find out how to tell the bees they aren't real - the flowers, I mean."

As Anna helped to re-position the hat on the child's head, the lump in her throat passed. It was time for an introduction.

"My name is Annie. What's yours?"

"My name is Elizabeth Lauren Henson, but everybody calls me Beth," she said just above a whisper.

With a wry smile, Anna held out her hand in greeting and said, "It's a pleasure to meet you, Elizabeth Lauren Henson. I love your hat! And bees only understand bee-talk, I think, but let's look for a book to make sure."

Perched on one of the little chairs designed for smaller bottoms and shorter legs than she now possessed, Anna looked through picture books with Beth for the next ten minutes. Anna was wondering where the child's mother might be when she heard the quiet voice.

"Well, there you are! I've been looking for you," the woman stated, seeming relieved as she approached them, carrying several hardcover books.

Anna was grateful to be interrupted, even from such a welcome pursuit as poring over picture books with Beth. She realized her entire left leg had gone numb as she tried, quite ungracefully, to rise from the elfin chair.

"Beth is very inquisitive and persistent," the woman explained. "I suggested she look up the answer to her question while I browsed the grown-up section."

"I think your daughter is perfectly delightful. It was her hat that caught my eye. Beth and I have learned all kinds of things together these past few minutes. But I'm afraid we still don't have an answer to her question. By the way, I'm Annie."

"And I'm Stacey," said the woman, extending her hand. "Thanks for helping my birthday girl. She's six years old today."

"Say," Anna said impulsively, "could I interest you two ladies in some ice cream? Six is a big birthday, and something tells me a little girl with such a fine hat deserves a reward after all this research."

Anna grabbed a paper as Stacey paid for her books, and the three of them strolled up the street to the ice cream parlor. The women talked while little Beth courageously tackled a double-decker chocolate cone that seemed almost as big as she was. She finished with a beard of brown, accompanied by a bib to match.

Gobbling the last of her dripping cone, Beth rummaged through her backpack and with sticky fingers, pulled out an iridescent blue plastic wallet.

She removed a photo of herself in the midst of a group of children, gathered around the U.S. President, of all people. They were sitting at the very same white wrought iron table, perched on red and white striped cushions and eating ice cream cones. All, including the head of state, displayed big chocolate smiles and sunburned noses.

"Look, there's the President of America, Annie, with me and all my friends. He likes ice cream even more than me. I know 'cause he told me so himself last summer when he came to visit us."

Anna smiled at the little girl and said, "You know the President has a very important job, Beth."

Beth scrunched up her face, tilting her head to one side. She glanced first at her mother and then said, "Well, I guess so. Do you have an important job, Annie?"

Anna hesitated before answering. "I never thought of my job as important, Beth; necessary, perhaps, but not important. Now, your mom has a really important job, even more important than the President! I believe moms have the most important job in the world. Sometimes, Beth, people forget just how special and important a job it is."

Anna felt Stacey's eyes on her as she stood at the counter to pay for the ice cream. As they walked toward the Explorer, the woman started fumbling through her bag of books. She pulled one out, checked the cover, and looked inquisitively at Anna. "You're her. I mean this is you, isn't it?" Stacey pointed to Anna's picture on the back cover.

"Yes, that's me, second book actually. The photo on my first is much more flattering," Anna said awkwardly.

Stacey became serious. Eyes filling, she reached over and touched Anna's arm.

"Dr. Carroll, I can't thank you enough. You don't know how you've helped me. Your first book changed my life. Could you...would you sign this book for me, please?"

Always surprised and humbled when this happened, Anna had still not gotten used to the fact that people actually read and benefitted from her advice. Maybe people do listen after all, she thought.

As she autographed the book and regarded the little girl, Anna said, "Stacey, I'm the one who should be thanking you. You and Beth have brightened my whole day." Anna gently re-positioned the floppy hat on the little girl's head and squatted down again to look into the child's eyes.

"Happy Birthday, little lady, and don't you worry about those bees. You have a very strong sense of yourself, and believe me, those bees will know it. You just tell them your name is Beth, and that your friend Annie says they aren't allowed to bother you. They'll understand."

She felt Stacey's eyes on her again as she got into the Explorer, but when she looked over to wave good-bye, Stacey was busy reading what Anna had inscribed in her book.

"Take good care of yourself and Beth," she had written. "She needs her mother - now and always. Godspeed, Anna Carroll."

Anna drove up Main Street, the tears trickling down her cheeks meeting the smile that was beginning to form on her mouth.

10

Lessons to Learn

he phone was ringing as she opened the back door of the house. Without thinking, she picked it up, instantly regretting the reflexive action. Regret turned to relief when she recognized Chris' voice, and figured he was checking up on her.

"I know I promised I wouldn't call, but Charly insisted," he said. "You know what a little worrier she can be."

"Sure, go ahead, big guy. Blame it on a ten year old. Why can't you just admit you were too curious to leave me alone?" Anna replied with a smile.

"No really, Annie, it was Charly's idea. Here, talk to her."

"Hi honey," Anna said as she filled the kettle with water. "So what's going on down there?"

"Well, Annie, Dad said that maybe you were lonely and we should check up on you. It's been a boring weekend here, although Dad did finally get rollerblades, and we went skating down Ocean Boulevard in Fort Lauderdale. Dad was the oldest guy on skates and he did pretty good." Anna heard Chris groan.

"Well, I'm doing fine here, Charly, and I appreciate your concern. Let me talk to your Dad again, will you?"

Charly's little voice dropped to a whisper, "I wasn't worried about you, Annie, but you know Dad."

Anna smiled as Chris got back on the line. "So Charly was concerned, huh?" she teased him. "Why can't you just say what's on your mind? And, honestly, Chris, rollerblading at fifty! What are you trying to prove? Haven't you spent enough money on those knees of yours by now?"

"It was worth it, Annie. Charly had a great time."

Chris had been divorced for five years now, and the wounds were still raw. The marriage had been a good one until his consulting business took off. It was hard to say whether success changed him, or whether all the nights and weeks away drained the soul from that union, but Anna felt it was one of saddest endings she had known. He had seen her through a few failed relationships as well, and had been her mainstay many years earlier when she herself divorced. Does success and self-fulfillment have to come at such a price? Is it possible for two bright, evolving, talented and ambitious people to sustain the journey through life together, each optimizing the gifts they had been bestowed? Anna and Chris spent more than a few hours discussing and debating those very questions over the years. Since his divorce, however, their conversations became less philosophical and more and more personal. The relationship took on yet another dimension, one which was never discussed, but increasingly ever-present.

The loud whistle of the tea kettle summoned her. As Anna poured boiling water into the thermos, fine dust from the low-cal hot chocolate mix wafted up and triggered a sneeze.

"You're not catching cold, are you Annie?"

"I'm fine, Chris," she said, smiling again at his not too subtle attempt to hide his concern about her. "In fact, I'm on my way out to Menemsha to watch the sunset. It was raining this morning, but the sun is out now. And, yes, it's cold. I'll tell you all about it next week. When are you back in town?"

"I should be back by Wednesday. Let's have lunch on Thursday. The agent called about the book, and I told her we'd have a proposal ready by the first of the month. Hope that's okay with you."

"I really haven't thought about it, Chris. When is the first of the month?" she asked, as she scanned the kitchen for a calendar.

"Annie, it's ten days from now," he said with a slight note of impatience in his voice.

She heard the irritated "get a grip" tone in his voice, but after the strange, though wonderful day she'd had, her mind wasn't really on work.

"We'll talk about it on Thursday, Chris. Thanks again for calling. Bye!"

The hot chocolate made, Anna ran upstairs to change those sandy socks and put on a warmer sweater. She had glanced at the tide table and noted that sunset was at four-twenty-eight. It was three-thirty, and she realized the timing couldn't have been better if she had planned it.

Anna had to put the visor down on both the driver and passenger sides of the Explorer as she drove into the setting sun to the little fishing village of Menemsha. Some of the most beautiful sunsets in the world could be savored from this remote little village. The place absolutely bustled in the summer, with fresh fish trading hands almost as soon as it was caught and cleaned. The little fish markets that lined the pier sold and prepared the best fish Anna had ever eaten. She figured if she were that impressed, then the place truly was the best anywhere, maybe even on earth. Anna enjoyed fresh catch from the Florida Keys regularly and year-round. If it wasn't from those crystal blue waters of the Florida straits, she was eating the day's catch from places such as Sebastian and Stuart, the not so well kept secrets of Florida's Treasure coast. Always partial to shellfish, especially lobster and clams, she was certain you could find no better than the catch of the day brought into Menemsha.

Sunsets were always spectacular, the purple and scarlet "sailors' sky" caressing the horizon, providing a vivid backdrop to the few tug and fishing boats remaining on the rippling water, which lapped gently against the rocky, craggy shore. A finer study in contrasts could not be found.

But there would be no fish, let alone activity today, she thought, as she turned onto the North road and began to drive across the rolling hills through Chilmark. Arriving at the village at three-fifty-five, she drove the Explorer to the edge of the beach and noticed the one lone truck that had preceded her. A woman with nearly luminescent white hair stood at the foot of the jetty with two young children - a girl and boy dressed in identical bright blue windbreakers trying in vain to chase down several sea gulls attempting to perch nearby. The children appeared to be oblivious to the wind and cold. As the woman turned and waved to Anna, a ray of the setting sun glistened through her hair, creating a glow so bright that Anna blinked. Anna smiled and waved back. Even off-season visitors are friendly, she thought. She turned off the engine and got out of the Explorer.

The wind whipped across her face, almost smarting it was so cold. Anna had trouble connecting the two ends of the zipper to her parka, so she turned her back to the wind. She put the hood of her parka up and pulled the little strings so that her face was partially protected. The sun was a brilliant red and barely kissing the horizon as Anna again turned toward the beach. In the glow of the sunset, she caught a glimpse of the now familiar man pedaling his bike toward her.

He pulled up next to the Explorer and joined her as she

braced herself against the wind.

"I knew you'd be here," he said, "so I thought I'd join you if you don't mind."

Together they braved the elements, struggling to reach the water's edge. "It's just too windy and cold out here," she said, as she reversed direction and scurried toward her vehicle. She hoped he could hear her over the howl of the wind. "Come join me inside where it's warm," she said, hopping behind the wheel.

Once inside the Explorer, Anna turned on the engine so she could get the heat running and stop shivering. The two of them watched the sun in its final moments, a red ball slipping slowly into the sea, as the steaming chocolate created a mist on the windshield.

"Endings and beginnings," Anna said aloud as she looked over at her companion, "that's really what life is all about, don't you think?"

Those comforting eyes looked back at her, and he nodded and said, "Yes, but it's really what happens between the two that makes a life meaningful. There really is only the moment, Annie, a perpetual now, if you know what I mean. So many people go through life focused on the openings and closings, goals and accomplishments, they miss the whole point of being here. We all have lessons to learn, Annie, and only a set amount of time in which to learn them. It could be five years, forty years or eighty-nine years. Just look at what you've learned today, since sunrise and this moment. In just one day, you've reviewed your life, and given yourself permission to feel both the joy and the pain of the connections in your life, and you've actually made some new ones - connections, I mean."

Playing with the steering wheel, Anna said, "I've been thinking a lot about the transitions we have to make in life, not just following abrupt, unwelcome change, but the every day, every week adjustments that gradually remold us into the evolving adults we become. We really are just 'works-in-progress', aren't we?"

"So many of my clients," she continued, "come to me suffering from stress or burnout, really flip sides of the same coin, but they resist taking any time to reflect and focus because they are afraid of the view. I realized today that in my own way I've been doing the same thing. I never stopped after my own surgery. I continued writing, speaking, actually increasing my workload in the months before Beth died. In a way, the busyness dulled my pain."

"Even those last weeks when Beth and the girls, and then Tom, were in my river house, I kept working. I only stayed with her for her final two days. I wasn't consciously avoiding being there, and she wanted me to go about my business as much as I could. I felt it best she have the most time with her husband and her girls. But today I realized I never really got to say good-bye to her. All the memories of a lifetime, and we never got to review them together."

She looked at him somewhat surprised at what she had just heard herself say. The lights went on in the truck next to her, startling both of them. It was dark now; the moment had passed. The ending of the day was gone in a brilliant blaze of light.

"I still have places I need to get to tonight, and people I need to see," he said. "Could you drop me at Bettlebung Corner on your way back?"

"Sure." Anna got out of the Explorer to help him with the bike, but it was already on the roof of the vehicle before she could reach the other side.

He was silent as Anna drove along the unlit road connecting the two sides of the island. Anna didn't want to interrupt his thoughts, especially after he had been so respectful of hers. As if he were reading her mind, he turned to her and said, "Maybe it would help you to write down how you feel about what happened today, Annie. It used to work for me."

She was quiet as they continued along the dark road. "I think I'll write a letter to Beth," Anna said, as she pulled in front of the old church at Bettlebung Corner. "Are you sure you'll be all right out here? It's very dark," she said, noting for the first time that his clothes were an odd shade of blue and didn't look too warm.

"I'll be just fine, Annie, and I think the letter is a good idea. It may seem strange at first, but trust me, it helps. I hope I will see you tomorrow before you leave, but, if I don't, it only means I ran out of time."

"Thanks for listening," she said, and he had closed the door before she realized she again had forgotten to get his name. She thought it was strange that he seemed to be aware of her plans, since she didn't remember saying anything to him about when she planned to leave the island.

11

Washing Away the Pain

As she pulled into the drive, Anna silently swore at herself for not thinking to leave any lights on. She flipped on the Explorer's high beams and shined them on the back door. As she reached inside the kitchen door for the switch, she noticed that there were no lights on at the Duffy's either.

Once the kitchen was illuminated, she turned off the Explorer's lights and gladly retreated to the house. Looking at the clock, she saw it was a little past seven o'clock. Suddenly, as if the time gave her permission, she realized she was ravenous. But she was also feeling quite sandy, so the shower came first.

Anna stood in the huge, glass-enclosed shower and let the hot water beat onto her back. She turned very slowly, slid down the wall, wrapped her arms around her legs, turned her face towards the pulsating stream, and began to contemplate the day. Anna had always concealed or camouflaged her deepest pain, keeping it very private. As she reflected on the day, tears filled, then dropped from her eyes, becoming one with the water streaming down her face. Anna sat weeping under the waterfall, wondering how many people retreated to a shower stall hoping the warm water would wash away their pain.

"Why is it that we only let go in private? Why are we so afraid of going public with our pain?" she wondered aloud as she stood and turned off the faucet.

Anna had spent years helping her male clients get in touch with their feelings, and working with women to understand theirs. She found men and women to be so different in so many ways, but so similar when it came to the important things. All just struggling souls stuck in these funny looking physical forms, trying desperately to make some sense of it all. That is, those who allow themselves to think about or question the meaning of life, let alone death. Thinking back to earlier in the day, she remembered how he wept along with her as she exposed her soul. He had touched her heart and soul in a way that no one ever had. Who is he? she pondered, drying herself with the big white towel.

The bathroom had more mirrors in it than Anna had in both of her houses combined. Staring at her reflection in this room of mirrors, all Anna could see were her three scars. She had two barely visible incisions, one on each breast, while the fiery pink "bikini" line was just starting to fade. These scars, like pain, were permanently etched into her body, yet expertly concealed from view.

Anna knew all too much about cancer. She had been through the drill more than once, undergoing mammograms yearly since her early thirties. Her first breast biopsy was the hardest, and that scar was the longest. Kind of fitting in an odd way, Anna felt. She was too young, she had thought at the time, to be dealing with this. She remembered how her sweaty hands trembled as she sat in the surgeon's office listening to his litany of cancer statistics and treatment options. The experience had left her shaken to the core.

The second biopsy on the opposite breast occurred when she turned forty. This time it was done as an out-patient procedure, more a testament to the ever rising cost consciousness of medical care than significant advances in technique. However, she had a different surgeon, a slightly better looking scar, and no cancer. She went alone to the hospital, took no medication, except for the local anesthetic during the procedure, and went against hospital policy and the nurse's judgment by driving herself home.

Anna had struggled for more than a decade trapped in that limbo of uncertainty suffered by so many women. Like most in her shoes, she courageously endured and faced the ever present reminder of her mortality, utterly alone. She never talked about it, rarely thought about it, but all the time was conscious of the threat. Every once in a while, Anna would find herself in a restaurant or department store, mentally calculating the numbers of people present who were struggling or suffering with cancer. That reality infuriated Anna more than it scared her. She told herself it was morbid and unnecessary to entertain such thoughts. So Anna pushed those thoughts out of her head, except for the one morning each month when she slathered her hands with soap and carefully examined each breast for lumps.

Despite it all, Anna always figured the odds were in her favor. When the ovarian tumor was discovered during a routine doctor's visit, she wasn't so sure. Of course, it didn't help matters any that two of her friends had died from ovarian cancer in the previous ten months. It was now round three for Anna. Her mother had not said that good things happened in threes. More importantly, her mother was dead, so Anna had no one to ask.

Anna had always been more terrified of cancer of the ovary than she was of breast cancer. It made no sense, really, she just was. Perhaps it was because of Gilda Radner. Both Anna and Beth were devastated when Gilda died. It was almost as if they knew her, maybe because in a way they did, and Anna, in particular, felt it was so unfair for someone like that to die so young.

Beth was the only one who knew how terrified she was of ovarian cancer. Beth certainly had more than Anna's fears on her mind at the time, leaving Anna to sort through her feelings on her own. Anna felt it was the strangest week of her life, that week between tumor detection and tumor removal. Despite all her practice with living with dread and fear of cancer, this was different. If someone like Gilda could die from this silent killer, at so young an age, then so could she. Again, Anna thought, cancer changes everything.

"It won't be malignant, Annie," Beth had said over the phone, "you have too much left to do."

Beth had been right. Anna ended up having painful abdominal surgery and lost all her reproductive organs. But she did not have cancer.

It wasn't that Anna didn't think about her good fortune; she did, all the time. She still couldn't imagine going through all that surgery and having it be only the beginning of treatment. It was that she never focused on the hysterectomy part at all until after Beth died. Anna figured the odds had been in her favor three times now, but, as any women who has experienced this surgery will tell you, it hurts. It hurts like hell for a while, and it hurts in your heart for a long time.

People say the stupidest things, Anna thought to herself. As a psychologist, she figured she had the right and the credentials to believe this to be true. After all, she had spent years counseling victims of the stupid, hurtful, even cruel verbal attacks from mothers and fathers, husbands and wives, children and siblings, teachers, bosses and co-workers, nurses, doctors, and religious and political figures. As she got older, Anna was less and less convinced that people were really as stupid or clueless as they tried to appear when caught hurting another person, or group of human beings, with their words.

She knew in the scheme of things she had been pretty lucky. So when some of her very educated, quite intelligent friends, colleagues, even her family, rendered their unsolicited opinions about the uselessness of the organs she had just lost, Anna pretty much dismissed it as anxiety over the situation, or relief that she did not have cancer. But, as she stood full face looking at her body with its scars, Anna started to feel quite angry, then hurt, and finally very, very alone. No one could ever know the meaning of this event in her life. That's not what bothered her. But were they really so stupid they thought there was none? As she traced the scar with her fingers, tears fell like raindrops on the cold white tile floor.

"Beth, you never did tell me what it is that I have left to do," Anna said through her tears.

A loud ring penetrated the silence and, since Becky and Michael had a phone in the bathroom, Anna's hand instinctively reached for the receiver. By the time she picked up, the answering machine had kicked on, so Anna very carefully replaced the phone back on the hook. She didn't want to talk to anyone anyway.

Anna blew her hair dry, then pulled on a pair of blue tights and her favorite baggy, fleece-lined sweatshirt. By habit, she put back in the small white pearl earrings she always wore, and went downstairs to fix herself something to eat.

12

A Whispered Prayer

The message light was flashing on the answer machine on Michael's desk. She made a mental note to check it before she went to bed. She changed the discs in the CD player, and started toward the kitchen when the sounds of Smokey Robinson filled the room. Some people never age, she thought, as she began moving along with the rhythm.

As she opened the refrigerator to get the wine, the bottle of capers caught her eye. That's when she knew what she'd make for dinner.

"What would you like for dinner, Annie?" Beth asked, once they had been seated at the restaurant recommended by the young American tourist. They relaxed on bistro-style chairs topped with bright blue and white checked cushions. The menu was posted on a blackboard directly above Anna's head.

They had never expected to find such a delightful cafe on the ground floor of the Louvre. But they had, after an exciting, but exhausting afternoon meandering through the museum. It was one of those times when Anna wished she had paid better attention in college. She and Beth took an Art History course in their last semester at the University of Maryland to fulfill some requirement. Anna relied on Beth's notes and memory for detail, as she rarely attended the lectures. Springtime was not to be wasted, Anna would tell Beth, as she went off to the driving range to practice her swing.

Unfortunately, the final exam consisted of slides, not questions, and most of the photographs the professor showed were his own and not from the textbook. The credit was all Beth's. It was totally due to her extraordinary ability for detail and description, and her dedication and insistence in making her friend study at all, that Anna got a C. At the time, Anna's only concern in getting a decent grade was to ensure her entry into graduate school.

Back then she never anticipated having an interest, let alone a passion for art. But here in Paris, the City of Lights, how could she not? Anna now regretted she was so ignorant of the culture, background, and artist's stories lending color and life to each masterpiece.

It had been Beth's suggestion to tack Paris onto that special British retreat the two had enjoyed just three years ago. They had weathered the hectic drive on the M-2, pausing to ramble through the sites they had read about in Canterbury Tales, as they hurried on their way to the Hovercraft that would take them from Dover to Calais.

Anna and Beth rode the train from Calais to Paris, where they would be staying in a very posh hotel on the Right Bank. Neither of them had ever been to Paris before, and Anna had been prepared not to like it. So many stories about the French people, from both her British and American friends, made her wary of the trip. Once they were settled in the hotel, however, and started walking down the Champs-Elysées, Anna fell in love with Paris. No matter that it was bitter cold and overcast, hardly the April in Paris depicted in all the brochures, Anna absolutely fell in love with the city. While London had theater, Paris had, well, everything else.

Anna and Beth wandered around Paris from dawn to midnight for three days, seeing more in that time than most people do in a week. They were debating whether their legs would carry them a few more hours so they could venture to the top of the Eiffel Tower. It was six o'clock and their last evening in the city. As they sat in the small cafe in the Louvre, they acknowledged that it was a bit early to dine by Parisian standards, but as Beth reminded Anna, who cared what people thought?

That morning Anna and Beth had gone to Notre Dame Cathedral. It was magnificent. They spoke in whispers, or not at all, as they walked on their tippy-toes like the two ten-year old Catholic school girls they once had been. Beth took off on her own while they were there, and Anna saw her kneeling at the foot of the statue of the Virgin. Neither one of them practiced Catholicism anymore; in fact, Beth had raised her girls Episcopalian. As for Anna, well, she meditated instead of prayed, and had her own concept of how and what to believe. But inside Notre Dame, Anna thought, everyone must feel Catholic.

Anna found an alcove harboring the figure of St. Francis of Assisi. There were no candles lit in front of his altar, so Anna settled in a chair and looked up and into the eyes of the towering figure. "I don't know if I'm here to keep you company, or because I feel badly no one has lit a candle in your corner, or because you were my favorite saint when I was in the seventh grade. But, I'm here, and that's all that matters."

Fumbling through her purse to find a coin, Anna continued

her dialog with the saint. "See that girl, I mean woman, over there having a conversation with the Blessed Mother? Well, she means close to about everything to me, and she has cancer. She is going to need a lot of help in the coming months, so please do what you can to see that whatever she's asking for, she gets. Thanks."

Anna dropped the ten-franc coin into the box and lit her candle. As she turned to leave, she looked into the eyes of St. Francis and whispered, "I could use a little help, too, if you can spare it."

As they walked outside and around the massive structure, trying to take it all in, Beth pointed up toward the spires of the Cathedral.

"Look, Annie, look, there they are. The famous gargoyles."

Anna figured Beth thought she'd forgotten the significance of gargoyles in gothic architecture, but she had not. She turned to her friend and said, "They are to keep the evil spirits away from the Church, remember, Beth?"

Beth looked sadly at her friend and said, "I could use one or two of them looking out for me right now."

"Well, we'll see what we can do about that," Anna said. And Anna had made sure two gargoyles were perched on the headboard of the hospital bed before Beth was returned to her room following her breast surgery.

Although Beth tried valiantly to translate their choices from the menu on the wall, both of them were so tired they ordered with only a marginal comprehension of what they eventually would be served. The meal was delicious, outstanding actually, and brimming with capers. So, warmed by wine and food, they walked from the Louvre to the Eiffel Tower and caught the elevator to the top of the century old landmark.

Looking out over the sparkling lights of the city, Beth turned to Anna and gave her a hug. "Please help me beat this thing, Annie," she whispered in Anna's ear. Anna silently nodded as the two women held onto each other like two little girls bravely facing unseen monsters. As the two friends stood together in the cold brisk air, Anna prayed that the tears she felt stinging her eyes wouldn't freeze on her face.

It was close to nine o'clock when they left the spectacular tower and walked until they found a Metro Station. Beth and Anna ran to catch a train back to the hotel, laughing all the way. How was it possible that two forty-five year old women with all those letters after their names had no clue what a caper was?

Anna scoured Rebecca's kitchen and found what you would expect to find in the kitchen of a woman who had two homes, full-time help in each one, and who was on the Martha Stewart Preferred Reader list. There were more cookbooks in this one house than Anna had text and reference books in her office. Anna found an interesting and not too difficult recipe for linguine with pesto, pine nuts, and goat cheese, threw in a few other odd condiments she had never heard of, and topped the dish off with two dozen capers. One for each day since Beth's funeral. The dish was actually quite good, though a bit on the salty side, but Anna was committed to finishing off each and every caper. As she was cleaning up following the feast, Anna wondered what kind of person would have thought to have goat cheese, pine nuts, and capers in the refrigerator for a visiting weekend guest.

She changed the CD's back to Mozart, Beethoven and Debussy, then rooted in Michael's desk for some paper, that flashing light beckoning to her. Not now, she thought, I'll check it later.

Anna found a tablet of paper and, rather than use one of the rollerball pens with some cardiac drug advertisement on the side - another reason so many patients cannot afford their medications, she thought somewhat cynically - she rooted in her bag, and found her Montblanc. The pen had been a gift from her agent, and she used it rarely. I guess I'm no better than Michael, she thought to herself as she tugged the top off the burgundy implement. Who am I to judge him so harshly?

13

Expressions From Mind, Heart, & Soul

Anna found a Duraflame log and lit it. She had used most of the dry logs that Patrick had piled for her on the side of the fireplace. There were two fairly good size ones left, but she thought she might extend the life of the fire by cheating a bit with the packaged variety. She was craving a cappuccino, and she knew there would be a machine somewhere, so she set off to find it. Sure enough, Becky had one.

The machine was screeching as the milk started to foam, and Anna deftly coordinated the process. Cup in hand, Anna walked through the kitchen, glancing at the clock. Incredibly, it was already ten o'clock. Anna didn't feel at all tired as she pulled the afghan up onto her lap and took her first sip of the strong, steaming coffee. She stared into the fire, its flickering flames of blue, yellow and orange both mesmerizing and soothing her.

She had no idea how long she might have gazed before she began to write.

> *To my dear friend Beth,*
> *This has to be one of the oddest things I've ever done,*
> *writing to someone who is now dead, but somehow it*

seems to be the only thing left to do. I miss you already, Beth, and I know how much I'll miss getting those postcards and notes from you. Just think of how much fun you and I would've had with e-mail. In a way we were already connected in cyberspace, old friend...

"What do you mean by that, Annie?"

Too stunned to be scared, Anna looked up to see Beth sitting cross-legged on the cocktail table. Her floppy denim hat was perched on her head, as she flipped through one of those coffee table books Becky had stacked on top. Anna said through tears of happiness, "Beth, is it really you?"

"Of course it's me, you ninny, who else could it possibly be?"

Anna couldn't believe her eyes. Beth was actually here, in the room and ready to talk to her.

"Well," Anna said, as she put the pen down, "I guess I don't need to write anymore."

"So, what do you mean about e-mail, huh?"

"You know exactly what I mean, Beth. You and I could communicate without even speaking at times. We would just look at each other and know what the other was thinking or feeling. But forget about that, I have so many more important things I need to talk to you about. How long can you stay?"

Inside, Anna wondered why she wasn't sputtering with amazement over this visit from Beth. But the two of them were so close in life, why not after death?

"As long as you need me to, but only for tonight. I felt we left things unfinished, too, and I thought I owed it to you to come back, so I found John and here I am."

"John? Who's John?" Anna asked. "Should I know this guy?"

"And just who do you think you've been connecting with all day, Dr. Carroll?"

"Oh, THAT John! So that's his name. Who is he? What does he do for a living, Beth? He seems a little troubled, somewhat ambivalent in a way, but down deep I think he's a very peaceful man. The type of guy who really is at home with himself."

Beth was smiling and shaking her head. "That's my Annie, ever analyzing. Annie, John was the priest who officiated at my funeral. Don't you remember he came over to you when you were sobbing, took your hand, and helped you into the limo?"

Of course. It all came back to Anna now. That's why he seemed so familiar, and that's why he seemed to know things without being told. It was all starting to make sense.

"So, he's the friend of the Duffys, huh?"

Beth looked at Anna, then looked away at the fire.

"Cousin, actually. Remember the week we spent here last fall, Annie? I know you remember our conversation that day in Becky's kitchen when I asked you if I was going to die."

Beth had a kind of smirky smile on her face when she looked at Anna and said, "One of best things about where I am now is I get to know what you're thinking without asking. It's a whole new way of connecting. It is fabulous. If we have time, I'll teach you a few things before I leave for good."

"Anyway," she was serious now, "you'll recall I took a long walk that afternoon after we spoke in the kitchen. You had hit the nail on the head with what you said to me, Annie, my friend, so I set out trying to figure out what I had left to do before I moved on. That was one of the wisest things that has ever come out of your mouth, Annie. It really helped me go the next step. As I was walking past the Duffy's house, John was coming out of their back door, looking pretty upset. I guess we were two troubled souls who connected, because he asked if he could join me and I said sure, though I didn't know what kind of company I'd be. In any case, that's how we met."

"As we walked, I told him I was dying. It was the first time I said it aloud. I really hadn't even said it to myself. It was very liberating... saying it, I mean. He just looked at me and nodded. I had no idea he was a priest at that point, I just felt comfortable talking to him. So we walked for miles, and I just talked. I told him about my mother, and how lonely I'd been all these years. I cried when I told him about the girls. I felt so bad knowing I would be leaving them behind. I asked him what I could do for them and for Tom, too. He was so terrific, Annie. He listened and asked questions, and by the time the walk was over, I really felt at peace. That man helped me face my own death and some-how transferred strength to me to do all that I needed to this last year. Before we parted that afternoon, I asked him what he did. He told me he was a priest. 'Father John Duffy,' he said. 'You know the Irish, a priest in every family'."

Beth looked away from Anna and sighed ever so softly.

"I just smiled at him, shook his hand, and said, 'I should have known. Thanks.' Then when I felt that the end was really close, I called Becky and asked her to find him for me. I had decided to be buried as a Catholic, and I wanted to talk to him while I still could. And that's how he came to be at my funeral."

Anna was staring at the fire. It had worked its way down to just embers, throwing various shadows around the room. Beth was sitting next to her on the sofa now, but she wasn't as clear as she had been sitting atop the table.

"I had to come back, Annie, to see you, or rather for you to see me one more time. It wasn't that I forgot about you, or didn't think about you this past year, it's just that I had so many others that needed me. You are so strong, Annie, you always have been. I've always known what I meant to you, my friend. You don't have anything to say that I don't already know."

"I came back, Annie, to tell you what you meant to me. I can't even begin to imagine what my life would have been without you. You were my rock, my anchor since we were in the first grade, wearing those ridiculous beanies on our heads. And when my mother died when we were in high school, Annie, I died too. I don't think you have any idea how hard a mother's death is on a child unless you've experienced it. As I grew older, I grew stronger, but if I hadn't had you and that family of yours, I know my life wouldn't have been the same."

Beth was beginning to fade from Anna's sight, but her presence continued to fill the room.

"That's why Tom and I had the children so early. I think down deep I always knew I'd have less time, and I didn't want the girls to be as young as I was when my mother had to go. When I spoke to John that day, I told him I felt guilty that I'd even had children at all. That I was selfish to have brought children into this world knowing my family history. He told me that we all have a purpose or reason for being, and that my girls were here because they wanted to be, not because of me. I thought it was an odd thing for a priest to say at the time. It sounded more like something you'd say, but it made me feel a lot better. Anyway, Annie, you have given me a wonderful treasure chest of memories to carry with me through all eternity."

Anna's eyes were misting but she could still see a faint outline of her friend. Beth was glowing now.

"I can't stay with you too much longer, Annie. Before I died, John told me what he had been so troubled about that day. He said he was thinking of leaving the priesthood, that he felt unfulfilled and insincere in his work. He told me that afternoon walk changed his life, too, and he realized that our meeting was not at all coincidental. John said he had never really reconciled the losses in his life, and that he and I had connected for a purpose. He helped me find my soul and I helped him revive his. I realized during my last hours on earth that I had chosen this life I had, and I died knowing that losing my mother was all part of the lesson I needed to learn. I also died understanding that life is all, no only, about relationships, Annie. You and I have a connection that knows no boundaries. Just as my mother was and is a part of my soul, so are you. I love you, Annie."

Anna could taste the tears because she was sobbing now. When she wiped the tears from her eyes, she could barely see Beth's face. The room had a warm glow to it, even though the fire had gone cold. Anna reached out to her friend, but could only hear her say, "Don't be sad, Annie, I'm always with you."

Anna woke up gradually, not with a start like the morning before. Her face was wet and the box of tissues on the floor next to the sofa was nearly empty. She looked down at her lap and saw a blank sheet of paper. She lay very still for a long time, watching the soft morning light bring the room alive.

"Beth, you forgot to tell me how to communicate with our thoughts," Anna whispered aloud.

Somewhere in the back of her head Anna heard Beth's voice say, "You already know how to do that."

14

To Believe or Not To Believe

As Anna lay on the sofa, she struggled between her heart and her head. She wasn't sure what to believe or even what she thought she should believe. Was Beth's appearance in this very living room a dream? Or, truly, a visitation from beyond?

Up until now, Anna had always favored her left brain - that dispassionate, objective, scientific dimension of her character. Like most competent psychologists, Anna based her practice on a set of theories or beliefs about what makes the human person, personality, or character tick. Anna was Jungian trained, hence she viewed dreams as symbols or metaphors created by the unconscious mind.

"Sometimes dreams help us work out a current struggle, maybe even solve a problem," Anna had said more than once to her radio audience, "or they can be forecasts or ahead of one's conscious reality."

Carl Jung wrote about the "meaning coincidence" between the dream and waking existence. In other words, for a time our subconscious synchronizes with the conscious mind. Fairly standard thinking for a mainstream therapist like Anna. So, in keeping with her character and training, Anna began to analyze her dream as she took her shower that Sunday morning.

Of course that's what it was, a dream, Anna told herself. A very powerful, emotive dream in which her friend Beth appeared to her to bring some closure to her endless grief. Or was it instead an opening?

Anna had no idea how long she was in the shower mulling over her dream. She went over every word. At least twice. What did it mean? She was brought back when freezing cold water suddenly sprayed her body. She jumped out of the shower with a shout. Being acclimated to Florida, she had forgotten how fast hot water turns to cold in New England.

Anna quickly towel dried and dressed warmly for the trip to Gay Head. Wolfing down an English muffin, she quickly poured some coffee in her travel mug. In wonderful contrast to yesterday, the sun had risen and produced a beautiful, sunny, cold November day. The sun at her back, Anna smiled wistfully as she took in the stark beauty of the rolling hills, thick with trees, dappled with sunny clearings.

She always appreciated this ride up-island. If she hadn't known she was in the United States, she would have sworn judging from the scenery she was in western England on her way to Cornwall, or out on the Dingle peninsula in Ireland. The road lined with the stone hedges was missing only the slow sheep farmer strolling with his herd. It was quite deserted this Sunday, with only a few of the houses emitting tiny trails of smoke. Anna decided to take the long way around to the lighthouse once she reached the fork in the road at the tip of the island.

As she turned the Explorer onto the road paralleling the coast, Anna saw flashes reminiscent of the breathtaking drive along the Pacific between Monterey and Carmel. She could almost hear the seals barking out on the big rock off the

Monterey peninsula. Always moved by the view, she was mesmerized by its majesty. And today, with just a hint of mist sneaking back over the brown mounds of sand, the landscape was especially beautiful.

She knew she could pull into any one of the private beach accesses this time of year, but she didn't. Anna had always been respectful of people's privacy, maybe too much so. Somewhat of an odd trait for one who spent each day probing into peoples' psyches. But that was done, of course, at their request. So she drove the length of the road and pulled into the vacant lot next to the path leading to the beach. It was strange to see it so empty. Anna could not remember a time when she hadn't seen at least a bicycle hidden somewhere. But today it looked as though she was the lone visitor to this hallowed land.

Anna carefully navigated her way down the long narrow path riddled with mud puddles from yesterday's rain showers. Once on the boardwalk that would take her to the beach, Anna checked her watch. It was close to ten o'clock. Working backward from her flight time of two-twenty, she calculated she had about an hour and half left to do whatever she had to do as she walked along the cliffs to collect her thoughts.

15

Connections
From Beyond

A fter a day like yesterday, Anna wasn't sure if she had the capacity for any feeling at all. She wasn't tired, or sad, or confused, or relieved, or peaceful, or anxious, or anything. She just was. She walked forever, looking out at the water and then down at the sand, occasionally stopping to examine a rock or a shell. It was during one of those movements from stooping to upright that she caught a glimpse of a figure in the distance. He was walking toward her from the far side of the huge cliff. She knew instantly it was him.

Neither one of them changed pace or showed recognition. As he came fully into focus, her mouth turned upwards in a big smile and a feeling of joy filled her heart. She knew he felt the same way.

They met at the big flat rock, and without speaking, almost in unison climbed up, sat Indian style, and looked out to the sea. Her hand reached over and touched his, and she turned and looked into his eyes.

Anna would swear later they talked for at least an hour. They talked about everything. He told her all about his life, from childhood up to when he met Beth. He had been the middle of seven boys, born in the projects in Newark, New Jersey. John's father had been a hard-drinking truck driver.

"He probably did whiskey shots and beer seven days a week for fifty years. He never missed a day of work, had an accident, or even had a fight that I knew of," John said as he looked out to sea. "You would say he was a functional alcoholic, Annie, and he was, but back then we just considered it being Irish."

John's mother cleaned other peoples' houses in addition to her own, of course, never once complaining. She washed, starched and ironed all seven boys' shirts for as long as John could remember.

"What I remember was the rash we all got from too much starch," he said, as he pulled down the top of his turtleneck to show Anna the permanent etching around his neck. John shrugged his shoulders and said with a smile, "Those collars are probably why I entered the seminary. My mother told me it was sign from God, a stigmata of sorts. I figured it was training for the Roman collar I'd wear as an adult."

"You cared for your mother very much, didn't you, John?" Anna asked softly, as she saw the dampness and love in his eyes.

"Annie, can you imagine how hard that woman worked? Just think about the shirts alone. Seven boys each needing a fresh shirt each day, five days a week, for close to twenty years, if you figure that all of us were in school for at least that long between Adam, the oldest, to Sean. The Duffy boys, A to S, we were called. Adam, Frances, James, then me, Kevin, Patrick, and Sean. There are two lawyers, one physician, an architect, a priest, and a college professor.

"Two college professors, actually, if you give me two jobs." He grinned. "James is a biologist and teaches at St. John's in New York. Quite an accomplishment for two working poor Irish folks, don't you think, Annie? My father put food on the table, but my mother put the heart and soul into our home. I will never forget her hands, those raw, red cracked hands that slapped and soothed each of us into who we are today. She was, no is, a saint."

He looked at her as he smiled and said, "Now, don't start with that analysis of yours. I know what you're thinking. Irish men and their reverence for their mothers, and all that. She was a wonderful woman."

Anna smiled back, but didn't protest, because that indeed was what she had been thinking.

He told her how he felt the call to be a priest, all about his seminary years, the parishes he had served, and about the academic post he eventually earned. He had a doctorate, of course, and taught theology at Fairfield University in Connecticut. It was after his first few years there that he had begun to feel lost.

Anna observed him as he told her his life story and calculated he must be in his early fifties.

"I just turned fifty-two last month, Annie," he said with a smile. "And no, I really don't think it represented my 'mid-life crisis'."

"Will you stop reading my mind!" Anna laughed with him.

He was serious again when he told her about meeting Beth a year ago, and what she came to mean to him. "She reminded me so much of my mother. Such a quiet strength, such a determined character," John said gazing at the blue sky. "She was so much like the mother I want to remember. She died just three years ago when she was eighty, but her soul had left long before that."

Puzzled by the remark, Anna slowly turned and looked toward him.

"My mother was never the same, Annie," he said very softly, "after Kevin was killed."

There are moments in everyone's life when all of nature, our physical surroundings, just stops. There is some piece of news so shocking, or an experience so intense, usually in its horror, only very rarely in its beauty, that we literally freeze in the moment. A plane explodes in the sky, a building is leveled, a beloved leader is mortally wounded. Horrific moments revealed by a glance at a headline or the flip of a knob. News that shatters dreams, for victim and survivor alike; news that becomes frozen forever in our collective consciousness.

Each among us, if we live long enough, will experience such pain and shock at least once in our private lives. There will be some news, event or experience that sears through our essence to the very core of our being. A phone will ring, a letter will be delivered, a doctor or nurse will avoid our eyes, and our world will be forever altered in an instant.

Anna had experienced this feeling twice in her life before the moment she sat with Father John Duffy on the top of the flat rock at Gay Head. The most recent was when, just a little over eighteen months ago, her gynecologist had told her she had an ovarian tumor. The other, well, it was when Beth had handed her the letter from Kevin's mother.

Anna's heart stopped in her chest, the ocean stood perfectly still and the breeze ceased to flutter. Anna Carroll's world came to a complete halt.

16

Expressions From Eternity

Anna would not remember how long it was that she stared into his eyes.

"How long have you known?" she asked.

"I didn't really connect it all together until we were walking yesterday morning on Chappaquiddick," John said. "That's why I left you and walked away. The revelation came to me in a flash, and I just had to leave."

Anna was sure she was sobbing. There were no tears, just a pounding in her chest and in her ears. But she needed to hear what he had to say.

"Kevin was two years younger than me. He would have been fifty in September. He was the brightest of us all, the heart and brains of the family, and none of us have really gotten over his death either, Annie."

John was crying now. He continued, "I am so happy to know about you and him, and at the same time, feel terrible that none of us had any idea about the extent of your relationship. We knew there had been a girlfriend, of course, but Kevin always had a lot of girlfriends, never just one. I guess we should have known by the letter he had left for my mother in case of his death."

Anna slowly turned her head, looked down, and took an envelope out of his hand.

"I never saw the letter until mom died three years ago," John said. "She had kept it all these years in a small cigar box by her bed. There were a few other things in there, but it was this letter that moved us the most."

With trembling hands, Anna touched the paper as if it were made of fragile glass. She just held on to it for what seemed an eternity. He carefully and softly pulled each one of her shaking fingers back and took the letter out of the envelope and began to read:

Dear Ma,

I know you wouldn't be reading this unless you needed to, so I know all of you are in a lot of pain right now. But I need you to do something for me, Ma. There is a wonderful girl at school who needs to know what has happened. I'm sorry now I never told any of you about her, or her about all of you but, well you know me, I was never too good at doing the proper thing. Anyway, she needs to know, and it would mean everything to me if you were the one to tell her I'm gone.

Between you and me, Ma, I love her like nothing else in the world. I honestly thought I'd be lucky enough to beat this stupid mess that I got myself into, and I thought we'd be together forever. I thought I'd come home, go to law school, become a famous lawyer, and together Annie and I would have lots of kids and change the world at the same time. But it looks like God has other plans for me.

I'm sorry you never got to meet her, Ma. She is very smart and fun to be with, but what I love best about her is kind of crazy. It's that she doesn't give a hoot what people think. She has the rest of her life to live, and we've only known each other a short time, so instead of her, I'm telling you. She is the love of my life, Ma, forever and always, I just know it. I'm telling you this, Ma, because I love you too much to let you go on thinking I hadn't found her.

Tell all the guys I'll do what I can for you and them from up here. And tell Pop to stop drinking. That stuff will kill him one of these days.

Love always.

*Your son,
Kevin*

Anna would never remember how long it was before she was composed enough to say anything. And when she was, John told her the most wonderful stories of the boy-man she knew so long ago, for so short a time, whom she had loved with her entire being. Kevin had been twenty-two, and Anna only twenty, and she had never let herself think or fantasize about what their future would or could have been together had he not been killed. She had just pushed all the pain right out of her heart, and tried to get on with her life.

As she sat with John, looking into the sea, her eyes filled with tears as she allowed herself to see and feel the wonderful, tall boy with the curly black hair and sparkling blue eyes. She could smell him again and her heart filled with anguish and joy. Every fiber of her being ached and longed for him in a way she wouldn't have thought possible after so many years. For a brief, intense flash, Kevin was alive again in her heart.

Anna looked down at the paper in her hand, and whispered, "I loved him with all my heart, John, and when he died, a large part of my soul went with him."

As she said the words aloud for the first and only time in her life, a great sense of joy mixed with indescribable sorrow filled her soul. And in that moment, she knew, without having to think about it, that her life had been what it was because that was the way it was meant to be.

John and Anna sat on the rock looking out at the ocean for what seemed like a very long time. They spoke to each other in their thoughts and with their hearts.

Their tears eventually dried, leaving streaks and stiffness on their cheeks. Anna would look back on that day and know she would have stayed there forever had John not been the first to go.

"I have to leave now, Annie. It really is time for me to go. Meeting you has helped me make a very difficult decision. Words cannot express how happy I am to know you. Annie, remember today for the rest of your life, and know that you will be in my heart for all time. We have forever to sort this all out, but now I really must go."

Anna, still shaken by the experience, just sat and watched him walk down the beach, around the cliffs, and out of sight. She looked again at Kevin's letter, reading it another time or two, and became aware of a very gentle breeze softly stirring around her. With the wind kissing her face and ruffling her hair, Anna slowly closed her eyes, feeling and tasting the sea breeze and salt spray. She very carefully folded her letter and slipped it into the pocket of her parka. Taking a deep breath, she got up from the rock and readied herself for the hike back up the beach.

Retracing her steps in the sand, Anna was overcome with emotion. The weeping began again, this time even more wrenching than before. Was it that she felt so alone after the solace of his company? Or was it exhaustion from feeling her pain and her grief?

Anna reached into her pocket for a tissue, and in that same instant, saw Kevin's letter fall to the sand. Stunned, she watched it skip along the water's edge. She quickly ran to grab it, but just as her fingers grasped at its edge, the letter was caught in a gust of wind. The paper soared up into the sunlight. As if in a trance, Anna felt the muscles in her arm and hand tense as she reached for those words that had so touched, yet pained her heart. Kevin's letter rose even higher toward the clouds, far beyond Anna's grasp.

With a moan of frustration, Anna sank despondently to the sand. She sat there staring after her letter, helplessly watching as it gently drifted to the sea below. The paper first rode then surrendered to the rhythm of the ocean. Anna stood up and wandered into the water, oblivious to the cold waves pounding at her feet. She watched as Kevin's words disappeared into the sea.

As the letter slowly faded from her sight, a very strange sensation came over Anna. She felt the wounds that had just opened in her heart and soul slowly close, then permanently fade away. And, once the raw shock of this revelation had sunk into her awareness, she experienced a peaceful knowing that made all the pain go away.

It wasn't until she was on her way back on the North Road that she realized John had walked toward the lighthouse, not the other way to the road.

Anna pinched her arm more than once on that ride back to Tisbury. Exhausted from the experience, she began to focus on all the questions she wished she had asked him. She should have asked about Beth. Of course, she wanted to know a lot more about Kevin. But, she had questions for Father John Duffy, priest. Or were they questions for John Duffy, Ph.D., theologian? Questions for a theologian she could entertain; questions for a priest were too much for her exhausted mind to handle. She gave herself permission to relax and not think about any of it. She would call Becky in a few days when she had sorted things out, and find out how to reach John. He, too, was going to want to stay in contact with her now, she was certain of that.

Anna checked her watch as she pulled onto State Road. It was close to one o'clock. She'd be cutting it close as usual, barely making her flight, but this time she had an excuse no one would believe. This is a story that is mine and mine alone to keep, she thought, missing Beth more than ever. For a brief, fleeting moment Anna actually wondered if she might be losing her mind. She then looked down at the beginning bruises on both arms, examined her reflection in the window, and smiled.

"No, Annie, you are not losing your mind," she heard Beth say. "This weekend has just been an experience that your mind is having difficulty accepting."

Grief does strange things to folks, Anna thought, and accepted that feeble explanation so she could focus on getting packed and to the airport in time for her flight.

17

A Mother's Loss

*P*ulling back out onto State Road, Anna remembered that she had never checked the answering machine. Well, it was probably Becky or Chris, and if it was important enough, they'd get in touch with her later. She looked at her watch and saw that she had miraculously changed clothes, cleaned her muddy shoes and packed, in time to be on her way by one fifty-five. She was grateful it was November and not the summer tourist season, as she noticed her Explorer was the only vehicle on the road.

As she drove down the country road toward the little air-port, she remembered the stories her mother had told her about women whose lives had changed in an instant. Women who had lost husbands or children, in a time when it was not all that unusual or unexpected to suffer such a loss as part of life. Families were so much bigger then, Anna thought, and certainly much closer in a physical, if not emotional sense. Not that that was comfort to the survivors; the losses were still tragic and for-ever changed people's lives.

On Anna's street back in the fifties and early sixties, there were close to a hundred children of all ages, and all families had two parents, except for one where the father had died. All the mothers were at home, hanging wash, talking to each other over backyard fences, and creating all sorts of good smells in their shiny white kitchens. The sounds of children filled the long, hilly street from dawn to dusk during the summer, and the block came alive by four-thirty every afternoon during the school year. Everyone knew everyone else.

When school started each September, a little parade of sorts would start about seven-thirty in the morning. Children of all sizes and shapes used to march to the top of the hill in maroon and white uniforms. Every once in a while, you could see a splash of color, when the kids who were off to the public school joined the parade. The Catholic school kids all walked the three or so miles to school, while the "publics" caught a bus at the top of the hill. If they missed their bus, they would join the parade until they reached the next corner. Smiling, Anna remembered how she and Beth had been in the fifth grade before they realized that being a "public" wasn't the only other option in life. That was the way her world was back then, "publics" and Catholics, all playing together and living together in the little town outside Baltimore.

As she drove, Anna studied the same barren trees she had barely noticed just forty-eight hours ago when Patrick had been at the wheel. The weekend had resurrected memories which filled her now open and accepting mind. Where to go from here? Anna mused. As she was mulling this question over, Anna adjusted the rear view mirror, catching a glimpse of her reflection. As she began checking her face and hair, Anna recalled the story her mother had told her about Mrs. Dougherty. Over the years, Anna's mother told many stories as the two would stand side by side in the kitchen doing dinner dishes. But Anna never forgot the story about Mrs. Dougherty and her twins.

Mrs. Dougherty lived at the bottom of the hill with her eight children. She was the nicest lady on the street once, her mother told Anna, a fact which Anna verified with the older kids on the block. There were two sets of twins among the eight children, a very big family for such a young woman. Anna never thought of Mrs. Dougherty as young, and when she asked her mother about the sadness in the woman's eyes that even as a little girl of ten she saw, Anna's mother told her the story.

Mrs. Dougherty had beautiful, shiny black hair that would fly silkily in the wind as she walked with her twins up the hill to the park. One day, the older set, a girl and a boy just turned six, took off on their own and went down the hill, not up like they were supposed to, and got lost in the woods. There was a creek in the woods where all the little kids were forbidden to go. Someone later vaguely remembered seeing the children walking hand in hand into the woods about mid-afternoon.

They found the children at dinnertime, face down in the creek. Their bright blue windbreakers had drifted to the water's edge and were tangled in the branches of the thick growth lining the river bank. Mrs. Dougherty was never the same after that. The neighborhood children would whisper nervously as they passed her in the park. There she would sometimes sit, staring with empty eyes and clutching shredded scraps of faded blue fabric, remnants of a happier past.

Anna's mother had to turn her head and look out the kitchen window when she explained to Anna why Mrs. Dougherty was the way she was. And that, Anna's mother had said, was why Mrs. Dougherty had white hair at only twenty-eight years of age.

As the years went by, Anna learned more of the tragedy from which the once vibrant, beautiful young mother never recovered. Colleen Dougherty's crowning glory, her shiny black hair, had turned white that night she lost her eldest children, her first set of twins, to the rippling creek in the woods.

A lone tear trickled down Anna's left cheek as she turned at the sign with the arrow and little plane on it. Anna looked over at her reflection in the rear view mirror, checking to see if her hair might have gone white.

It was five minutes after two. Anna parked the Explorer, locked the keys inside for Patrick to pick up later, and hurried into the building.

18

The Glow of Enlightenment

"Good afternoon, Dr. Carroll. It's good to see you. I hope you had a nice weekend. Looks like it's just the two of us again."

Anna forced a tepid smile at the cheery young flight attendant and took her seat. The sun was high in the sky, shining so brightly it gave Anna an excuse to hide her eyes under dark sunglasses during the flight. While she was gazing at the peaceful clouds, Anna accepted a glass of water brought by the attendant. The flight was smooth and the skies were beautiful. Anna took sips of her water as she admired the heavens. It wasn't until the pilot announced that they were approaching LaGuardia and the young woman came over to collect the glass, that her earlier remark actually hit home.

"Excuse me," said Anna, "but I was quite tired on Friday and was not paying attention on our trip out to the island. What did you mean when you said a little while ago, 'Just the two of us again'?"

The flight attendant smiled. "Don't you remember, Dr. Carroll? You were the only passenger on the plane. I made some comment about it, and thought maybe I had offended you in some way. You never even looked up during the trip, even when I refilled your Coke. You seemed lost in the clouds, or deep in thought the entire way, so I just kept to myself, though I really wanted to talk to you. That's why I was so happy to see you this afternoon. I was hoping maybe I could talk to you today, but I can see that you still have a lot on your mind."

No other passengers? Anna fumbled with her sunglasses. She needed distraction. If she fully grasped the words she was hearing, she would start to panic. She was already more unsettled and off balance about her dream of Beth, let alone the revelation on Gay Head, than she cared to admit, even to herself. Now this.

Anna somehow answered. "Yes, you're right, I have a lot going on right now. I did have quite a weekend, thank you, and so many thoughts and feelings I need to sort out. But we have few minutes before we land, so tell me, what would you like to talk about?"

As the young woman began to speak, Anna breathed deeply, convincing herself the imagined companionship on the plane on Friday was not significant. That tap on her shoulder had been the flight attendant gently waking her from her reverie. And outside, well, she was so anxious and preoccupied, she had wished for the offer of assistance and confused it with the real thing. No big deal, Anna reassured herself, as she tried to focus on the young woman. The rest of the weekend was real, she had the bruises on her arm to prove it.

"...and so, Dr. Carroll, that's why your book helped me so much. After our flight together on Friday, I went to the book-store and bought your latest one. I bought two copies, actually, one for me, one for my mom. Could you please autograph them for me?"

Anna's logical internal dialog had the desired effect. She was cool, calm and collected. With her most professional author's aplomb, she took one of the books from the young woman's hands and said, "How should I inscribe this one?"

"Well, my mother's name is Leah, why don't you write in her book first?"

Anna wrote and signed the inscription.

As the plane continued its descent towards LaGuardia, the bright light of the sun began to fill the cabin. At first, Anna was almost blinded by the light as it reflected off the shiny window casings across the aisle. Slowly, however, the brightness faded and a soft white light radiated throughout the cabin. Anna felt a warmth and presence all around her, which relieved all remaining remnants of anxiety and confusion. It was only for a split second, but Anna could have sworn she saw Beth, sitting in the row across from her, beaming in her direction as she faded away.

Quite calm by now, her mind at ease and her heart filled with a newfound understanding, Anna looked up at the young woman as she took the second book from her hands and said, "Don't tell me. Your name is Beth, isn't it?"

The beautiful young woman with sparkling blue eyes said, "How did you know that, Dr. Carroll?"

Anna was smiling now as she looked between the clouds and replied, "Well, I guess you might call it a hunch, but in reality, an angel whispered it in my ear."

Anna winked and passed her the books, thinking about the true meaning of the words she had spoken.

The little plane landed smoothly and Dr. Anna Carroll was once again back on the ground.

19

A New Way of Knowing

*I*t was after midnight when Anna walked into her house. She was exhausted beyond belief, too tired to brush her teeth or remove her clothes. She just flopped on her bed and fell immediately and deeply asleep. The persistent ringing of her phone woke her, and as she reached clumsily for the receiver, she saw that it was nine-fifteen in the morning. It was her secretary on her private line.

"Anna, is that you? When I didn't hear from you last night or early this morning, I thought I'd better check to see whether or not you made it back to paradise."

Anna thought she had the best secretary in the world. The women were about the same age, but so different; in this case complementing each other perfectly, making for the best working relationship ever. Her secretary loved schedules, details, the practical and the routine. It had been a perfect match for close to five years. Ellie loved that Anna needed and appreciated her organizational skills. As a result, the office ran with incredible ease, despite Anna's constantly changing priorities, her messy desk, calendar and Rolodex, and the demands of her many and varied clients.

"Yes, I made it back, in body anyway, Ellie. Though my spirit is still on the Vineyard." Surprised at herself, Anna asked, "I'm not seeing clients today, am I?"

"No. Remember, Anna, we decided to give you the morning to rest, but you do need to be in here by two o'clock for a conference."

"I'll be there. I'm exhausted. It's a long trip to make for such a short time. I overestimated what I could do, as usual," she said as much to herself as to her secretary.

"Well, you know, I kind of anticipated as much, so I hope you won't be too upset that I canceled the rest of the week for you. I did run the idea by Chris, and he said he'd call you about it, but I guess he forgot."

The blinking light on the answering machine, Anna thought. "No, no, Ellie, it's great you cleared my week. You are too much! Are you getting psychic on me?"

"Me? No way, Anna! I just had a feeling you would need more than a weekend. I thought maybe you'd want to go up to Vero for a few days."

Suspecting a little collusion now, Anna thought back to the conversation on Saturday with Chris about the book and smiled. "I may just do that," Anna said. "I'll see you in an hour or so. We can go over a few things before my meeting this afternoon, and then I'll head on up the coast."

That afternoon Anna drove north on I-95 on a relatively cool evening for November in Florida. She turned on the CD player, opened the sunroof and felt the wind breeze through her hair over the uplifting sound of Gloria Estefan. Anna found herself smiling as she listened to the talented soulful voice recognized around the world. As she pulled off the highway and headed east towards the river, Anna realized this would be her first time in her river house since Beth died.

As always, Anna smiled as she walked into the little river house. She opened all the shutters and blinds, threw open the big sliding doors facing the river, and let the wind off the water blow all the remnants of death and sadness out of the house, and out of her soul.

Later, Anna strolled out to the end of her dock. Sitting on the bench, watching the mullet jump into the gentle waves, she tried to sort through her weekend. As she searched the river for answers, she saw a lone dolphin swimming against the tide. Mesmerized by the rhythm of his graceful stride, Anna thought it strange he was alone. Dolphins usually swim in pods, a group of family and friends who play and protect each other as they navigate the unpredictable seas. This one, this loner, was headed off on his own. As he reached the bridge, Anna could barely see his fading dorsal fin becoming one with the rippling waves of the river. Slowly and gracefully, he just naturally became one with the water as he continued on his journey beyond the bridge.

The ringing of the phone broke the spell. She walked quickly to the house, somewhat perplexed that she could even hear it, since the dock was a good 175 feet long. Very few people had the number for the Vero property, and she had no machine. Anna made it back to the house by about the eighth ring and heard Becky's voice on the other end.

"Annie, it's Becky. I wanted to make sure you got home all right, and that your weekend was all that you needed and wanted it to be."

There was a softness and depth to Becky's voice that Anna had never heard before, and it touched her in a very special way.

"I was going to call and thank you and Michael. Becky, my weekend was just indescribable. I was just out on the dock, trying to put the pieces of this puzzle we call life together."

They talked, on a new deeper level, and in a new way.

While Anna couldn't actually tell her what had happened over the weekend, she was able to somehow communicate the power of it all. As the conversation closed, Becky remarked something about the Duffy house next door. That reminded Anna to ask how she could reach John, but before she could, Becky said, "It's just so sad, Annie, it was just such a tragic weekend here. My heart goes out to all the family." Becky's voice broke as she continued, "John was loved by so many people, Annie. He was a truly remarkable priest."

What? What was going on? Anna's chest started to constrict, getting tighter with her deepening anxiety. She sank down on the big chair in her living room, grasping the phone with a now sweaty hand.

"Becky, what are you talking about?" Anna's voice was barely audible.

"Didn't you get the message we left for you over the weekend, Annie? I was too upset to call, so I asked Michael to. Saturday night he phoned to tell you there would be no activity at the Duffy's after all. We didn't want you confused up there all by yourself. It was Mary's cousin, John, Father John Duffy, you may remember him from Beth's funeral." Becky was really crying now, but she continued to choke the words out.

"John was on his way to the Vineyard for the weekend, too, like I told you. In fact, the accident happened about the time you were scheduled to arrive at the airport. He was hit by a drunk driver on the Connecticut Turnpike. By the time the paramedics arrived, it looked bad, but they got him to the hospital. Michael and every other available specialist stayed by his side all weekend. John's condition stabilized on Friday, and there were actually a few hours on Saturday when even the physicians thought he'd make it. But our hopes weren't enough. By sunset on Saturday they put him on life support. That gave enough time for all his brothers to come to his side."

Anna was weeping softly now, her hand covering the receiver of the phone. She felt she knew where this story was going and how it would end. Unaware of Anna's reaction, Becky was now over the worst of her tears. Her voice took on an eerie calm as she continued with the story.

"By Sunday morning, the entire Duffy clan had arrived, with spouses and offspring in tow. Michael and another doctor took John off life support around noon. Then each brother in turn spent a final moment with John. Sean, the youngest, brought his four year old daughter in with him. Michael said this was especially moving, watching the father and daughter say a tender good-bye. A few minutes later, with all the family gathered round, John took his last breath and was gone. Michael said it was a very peaceful death and that he had never seen a family of a trauma patient better prepared. But it still feels so tragic."

Anna sighed deeply, as Becky continued. "Annie, you know how 'in charge' Michael always is? Well, something else happened, and he's not quite sure how to deal with it. He even said he might want to talk to you about it."

"What happened?" Anna managed to stammer through her subsiding tears.

"Michael says soon after he pronounced the death, everyone moved into the hallway, leaving him alone in the room with John's body. Michael stood by the bed - he doesn't recall for how long. And then he felt a gentle tap on his hand and looked down to see a little girl with curly copper-penny hair reaching up to him." Becky's voice tightened, as if to suppress renewed tears.

"He picked her up, and she whispered in his ear, 'Don't be sad. John says it was time for him to go. He wants me to give you this.' And she handed Michael this perfect little sunflower."

"A sunflower?" Anna interrupted.

"Yes, Annie, a sunflower," replied Becky, with just a hint of impatience. "The child then leaned over the bed rail and kissed John on the forehead. Turning back to Michael, she said, 'John says to tell you that Annie can help you understand.' "

"Michael said he was touched and also perplexed, but in the following moments, what with having to say good-bye to the family, phone me with the news, and then finish his charts, he was too distracted to take it all in. But then, and this is so strange, he stopped the nurse in the hall, and they chatted about how wonderful John's family is. Michael showed her the flower and said how touched he was by this gift from John's niece. The nurse didn't understand, so he tried to explain. But she said, 'Doctor, you've had a long day. Why don't you go home and take it easy. You know that hospital policy restricts underage visitation. We bent the rules to allow Sean's daughter in with Father Duffy, but only because he promised to keep it brief. When I left the room with the family, I personally escorted the child outside to a neighbor waiting to take her home.' "

"So, Annie, will you talk to him? He's very unsettled by this and insists he knows what he saw and heard."

An unusual sense of peace and understanding enveloped Anna. She was standing now by the big sliding doors, staring out at the last bit of light from the day reflecting off the houses across the river. Her eyes were dry and everything very slowly came into focus. It was as if she had always known what she did now, as if close to fifty years telescoped into this one moment in time. The merger of logic with faith offered her a clarity of vision and understanding she would carry with her the rest of her life.

"Sure I can, Becky, but not just now. Give me until tomorrow or the next day, okay? And tell Michael not to question his experience. I believe him."

Becky started weeping again and said, "Oh, Annie. I'll tell him right now. I know you wouldn't say that if you didn't believe it yourself. You are, and always have been, such a good friend to us both. And it's just the three of us left now, isn't it?"

"I'm going to say good-bye now, Becky," Anna said calmly and softly. "I'll call you later, I promise."

"I just wished you could have known him, Annie," Becky said through her tears.

"But I do know him, my friend, I do," Anna whispered into the phone.

20

Anna's Treasures: The Gift of Loss

A nna had asked Ellie to take care of the details, and, of course, she did. So when Anna walked into the little restaurant in Jensen Beach to meet Chris for dinner on Thursday evening, she knew everything would be as it should.

Anna had spent Tuesday and Wednesday in another world. She cleaned her river house and spent hours poring over her old photo albums. She smiled and frowned, laughed and cried. I'm purging my soul, she thought to herself during those two days. She felt compelled to review and organize her past.

It was on Wednesday afternoon that she found the shoebox tucked under her bed. When she opened the box, she saw the floppy denim hat. And under the hat, Anna found two little maroon beanies with the emblem on the front, one had a "B" embroidered on the inside, the other, an "A." Anna smiled. She and Beth were always getting their St. David's beanies mixed up, and it had been Anna's idea to do the initials. Not that it really mattered, Anna just wanted an opportunity to show Beth some of the embroidery stitches her grandmother had taught her. And under the beanies, there were all sorts of things.

Beth left Anna her sorority key, the amethyst crystal rosaries she got from Sister Rosemary when she was the May Queen in sixth grade, pieces from the Monopoly game, including the deed to Boardwalk (finally, Anna thought), all her Girl Scout badges sewn with childish stitches on the long green banner, and many photos of the two of them taken with Beth's Brownie camera.

Anna smiled as she slowly reached for the stack of postcards. Beth had saved those messages that Anna had sent her over the years. There were postcards from San Francisco, London, New York, Portland, Tokyo, Sydney, Kauai and Frankfort. She had kept them all and wrapped them together with the black armband she had worn at their graduation in 1970. Anna's eyes misted as she reread the greetings she had sent to Beth over their adult lives. The mist turned to dampness, then to streams of tears when she opened the plain white envelope and slowly began to read:

My dearest Annie,

I hope you are happy, and no longer sad, by the time you find this "treasure chest" I've put together for you. The girls and Tom helped me. And I think doing it helped them. I know how much it helped me. I've left you a lot of things that I've treasured for years, including the pin I bought in London that week before my surgery. You may remember, there was a Celtic exhibit in Liberty's, and I was moved by both the beauty and meaning in the art.

Wear it, Annie, for the rest of your days, and may it give you the understanding and comfort it offered me.

I've tried my hardest (I better not write "damnedest," I am dying you know. Not exactly the best time to gamble with profanity!!) to get all the pieces in place for you. I've prayed for help to do that for quite a while, and John (I know you will have met him by now) has promised to do all that he can on his end. So, there really shouldn't be too much left for me to say that I haven't, or anything you didn't understand that you don't now.

My gift to you, dear friend, is what you already know. So go to it. I know you can. People will listen to you, they always have. And on the outside chance they don't, well, you never cared what people think anyway.

Remember, I'm with you always, and I love you for all time.

Your friend,

Beth

Anna slowly opened the purple velvet pouch and carefully removed an unusual, hand-crafted pin of fascinating swirls and knots. The pin was attached to a piece of parchment describing its art and meaning.

Celtic Symbols
Knotwork –
Eternal Journey

For the Celts, existence was a journey toward the sacred worlds of gods and goddesses which continued over many lifetimes before completing the search back to the divine source. This pin symbolizes the endless riddle of life through successive rebirths, with its intricate swirls and patterns reflecting the continuous search for eternal life. The interaction and intermingling of the knotwork conveys an acceptance of the many levels of existence in the universe, and a sense of being connected or knotted to all the mysteries of the cosmos.

Anna very carefully held the delicate pin against her heart before fastening it on her sweatshirt. And with this action, all the pieces of the puzzle of her life came into clear focus, creating a picture for Anna affirming all that she had just come to understand.

At the very bottom of the shoebox was a somewhat faded

and worn holy card of St. Francis of Assisi. Through her still moist eyes, Anna gazed at the inscription on the back of the card:

In Memoriam

Mary Elizabeth Farrell O'Neill

August 1, 1918 - August 31, 1962

Anna carefully put her precious mementos back in her treasure chest. She first called and got little Beth Henson's address on the Vineyard, then sat down and wrote her a letter. She enclosed a small picture book of the saints, which explained how St. Francis, friend of birds and animals, came to be known as the patron saint of the environment. The life of St. Francis, she wrote, would have all the answers little Beth ever needed about the bees, or any other questions she had about life, for that matter. Anna put the rosaries in her pocket and the hat on her head, and thought, or perhaps prayed, about what she had to say to Chris.

She hugged him tightly for a long time when he came to join her as she sat in the corner alcove of the small restaurant. Anna was very nervous; she had no idea what he was going to say or think. They ordered some appetizers and wine, and Anna very slowly began to tell Chris her story. All of it. She left nothing out. When she finished, the two left the restaurant and walked to the water's edge.

Chris looked over at Anna with glistening eyes. "I believe everything you've told me, Annie, because I know you and trust you. I don't understand it all, but somehow I know I will in time."

She took his hand and sighed deeply. They gazed silently at the pearlescent moonlight reflecting off the rippling water, creating sparkles and shadows that danced across the bay. She felt his arm encircle her waist, and she immediately returned the gesture. Anna could feel him breathing as she rested her head on his shoulder. Slowly, she turned and looked into his eyes.

"Thank you for believing me, Chris. You are the best friend I have, big guy. I love you, but you already know that, don't you? And by the way, I *do* care, very much, what *you* think." And she winked at him.

Anna and Chris spent the days and evenings, which turned into weeks, following Anna's weekend on Martha's Vineyard, just talking and listening to each other. They talked about their childhoods, their loves and fears. They talked about their successes, but mostly they talked about their failures and the lessons learned, and the ones that somehow passed them by. They laughed together, those incredible deep belly laughs where you almost feel sick, but you keep laughing because it feels good at the same time. They both cried until they thought they had no more tears, and then they cried some more.

Anna and Chris had a tough time selling the agent on their idea, but together they were an unbeatable team. They had recorded their sessions on Anna's little dictaphone, and they both listened to themselves for a second time, in a more detached, if not scientific way. They each took notes from the tapes, and then they compared them. And from those notes, they came up with a list of lessons. And then, together, they wrote their book. When their book came out the following fall, Anna and Chris were vacationing on the Vineyard with Becky and Michael.

On A Wing and A Prayer: Reflections on Love, Loss, and Renewal by Anna Carroll, Ph.D., and Christopher (The Coach) Hayden, was dedicated to Beth O'Neill and Father John Duffy. The cover portrayed an angel with sparkling blue eyes and copper-penny curls, standing in a field overflowing with vibrant sunflowers. If you looked close enough, you would discover a splendid bee perched on her shoulder.

The book, their first collaborative effort after twenty years of friendship, sold out of its first printing in less than a week and its second within the month.

Best of all, almost everyone understood what they had to say.

Reflections on Love, Loss, & Renewal

- Slow down and spend time with yourself. There is a pattern of swirls and connections in your life that only you can understand.

- Words aren't always necessary when trying to comfort the ill, injured, or bereaved. A gesture, a hug, a touch may convey the words you are struggling to find.

- Experiencing serious illness, injury, and/or loss changes everything, and that's as it should be.

- To help yourself or others, reach out. To heal yourself or others, look within.

- Loss is the ultimate personal experience. Face your loss - don't run from it. It is only when you embrace your pain that you can begin to release it - and to heal.

- The most important relationship we have in life is the one with ourselves. Yet it is relationships with others that teach us who we are. Tell those you care about how much they mean to you. Do it now.

- Everything you've experienced up to now in your life has just been preparation for what you're supposed to do next.

- Believe in the unbelievable, or at least consider it. Dream more and worry less.

- Success in life is best measured by the quality of our relationships and the lessons we learn.

- Understanding that death is part of life is just logical. Believing that death is really not an ending, but actually a beginning in disguise, takes faith.

Postscript

Dr. Joyce Brothers and Lois Wyse have written about it. So has Anna Quindlen. Yet the subject of friendship, its place and meaning in our lives, has actually received very little attention when we consider the importance this critical relationship has on our mental and emotional well-being. Like most folks, I hadn't given the subject much thought. Cancer brought me to an appreciation of many things these past few years, as I watched three of my colleagues, my friends, die. While each relationship had its own unique quality, I was struck by the impact these deaths had on me and how much I had taken for granted all these years.

I have always been blessed with a lot of friends. In fact, on a very personal level I realize that is how and why I wrote this story. I felt compelled to make a statement, both personally and professionally, about the importance of friendship as we face middle age. I have also been concerned these past few years as I observe how people, especially women, relate to one another in the workplace. I wrestle with what I believe has been lost or compromised these last two decades, as women have struggled to make their place in organizational life. In the drive to succeed at all costs, I am concerned that too many women have lost attachment to one another. It troubles me, and it saddens me. I created "Anna" and "Beth" and developed their relationship to illustrate what is truly important in life. "Beth" and "Anna" have a unique but very common life-long bond shared by millions of women across the globe.

Eternal Journey is my way of acknowledging and thanking my friends for always being there for me and for many wonderful and funny memories along my journey. "Beth" embodies the very best qualities of these women, each of whom continues to touch my life in memorable ways.

My friend, Regina Pakradooni, my confidante since childhood, provides Beth's sense of humor and devoted loyalty to Anna. Regina's sister, Anne, died when we were too little to understand, but not too young to know. I have watched and learned from Regina as she has struggled all these years to make sense of the loss of the little sister who was here for so short a time. She knows I felt Anne's spirit as this story came to life.

My friend, Janet Colesberry, my companion in grade school and Brownie Scouts, gives Beth her wistful tenacity and consideration for others in the face of serious illness. The hand-crafted silver and pearl pin Janet sent me, in appreciation for my support during her successful treatment for breast cancer, provided inspiration for the book.

My best friend in high school, Cecilia West, who lost her mother, Anastasia, to breast cancer during our sophomore year, gives Beth her spirit and her faith.

My friend and college roommate, Barbara Meyers, gives Beth her thoughtfulness and sense of organization, her patience and her pragmatism. Our three decade long friendship provides the inspiration for the respect and connectedness Beth and Anna have for one another, despite years between visits and months between phone calls.

My dear friend Bonnie Eyler, who also lost her mother, Elizabeth, to breast cancer, has seen me through the losses and triumphs of my adult years. Bonnie gives Beth her penchant for surprise, and her logical belief in the sensibilities of the universe. It was Bonnie who provided the title for the book.

My friend, Marion Gunter, who died from breast cancer in 1990, was a spirited being who truly "lived in the moment." Marion's zest and passion for life up to her final breath was an inspiration to everyone who knew and loved her. In the grip of terminal illness, she maintained a strength and determination that astounded and touched me. Marion's spirit is immortalized in these pages.

My sister, Barbara Quigley, gives Beth her beautiful red hair and her persistence, if not stubbornness, in the face of adversity.

I am indebted to each of these remarkable women for the experiences and memories that helped bring "Beth" to life.

My niece, Lauren Elizabeth, provided the inspiration for "little Beth." Lauren's curiosity and sense of wonder about nature provided material to weave into this story. Just before her seventh birthday, on a beautiful June day atop Catalina Island, she asked me how to speak with bees, while wearing her denim hat. Lauren embodies the very essence and spirit of little girls from all time.

In my years as a nurse and nurse practitioner, I cared for many terminal patients. Like many nurses, I have had a special connection with more than a few. I have been fortunate, perhaps blessed, to have known such spirited souls as they prepared for transition. The learning and insight into the human spirit gleaned from these special individuals has brought me to an understanding and acceptance of pain and loss for which I am eternally grateful. In that sense, this story, while less than fact, is certainly more than fiction.

About the Author

Dr. Carol Hutton is the founder and principal of Hutton Associates, an international consulting practice in management, leadership, and organizational change. Dr. Hutton's specialty is process consulting - guiding clients to seek solutions by asking questions while challenging them to "learn how to learn" in new ways. Her clients have included American Express, Lufthansa German and Northwest Airlines, Columbia/HCA, and Heart of Kent Hospice in England.

An Adjunct Professor in the School of Business and Entrepreneurship of Nova/Southeastern University, Dr. Hutton teaches graduate courses in Organizational Development and Leadership/Management. She holds a doctoral degree in Adult Education from Florida State and nursing degrees from Yale and the University of Delaware.

Dr. Hutton has published numerous articles and book chapters related to health care, adult education and management. *Eternal Journey* is her first book.